Autobiography of Miss
perspective of an Africa
Faulkner has told the sto

MW01008992

ern aristocracy, so too does Gautreaux tell a story of the South,
provide *a* voice of Louisiana. None of these writers (not even
Faulkner) presumes to be telling *the* story of the South, and each
of their voices, with all their distinct issues as well as areas of
common interest, reminds us that there are numerous stories to
cover when "tell[ing] about the South." Tim Gautreaux's voice,
relatively new in the mix, allows a welcome expansion of our
understanding of the variety of cultures that make up the
South—indeed, that make up even the single state of Louisiana.

Historical novels (even Gautreaux's first novel, set in the
1980s, might be considered such) and traditionally structured
short stories give Gautreaux's fiction a surprisingly fresh perspective beyond the new voice of the Cajun that he provides. He
resists the experimental form so common in the work of some of
his postmodern and contemporary peers: "I see the short story
not primarily as an intellectual endeavor, but as a cultural arti-
fact tightly bound with a necessary narrative structure" (Levasseur and Rabalais, 24). His stories break out of the blue-collar
tradition that John Barth describes as "terse, oblique, realistic or
hyperrealistic, slightly-plotted, extrospective, cool-surfaced" fiction labeled as "'K-Mart realism,' 'hick chic,' 'Diet-Pepsi minimalism,' and 'post-Vietnam, post-literary, post-Postmodernist
blue-collar new-early-Hemingwayism.'"[25] Gautreaux's fiction
relies heavily on theme, characterization, and plot—that is, traditional storytelling elements that slow the reader down to a savor-
ing pace. And Gautreaux prefers the voice of the uneducated
speaker over the intellectual perspective, noting that "some intellectuals think too much and they like to strike poses of darkness

and brooding because they think that's what they are supposed to do. . . . If you're educated you're supposed to be pessimistic. I've become very pessimistic and cynical about pessimists and cynics. That's one reason I like blue-collar people. With all of their shortcomings and biases and pent-up angers, most of them understand the value of being good-natured and having a good time" (Levasseur and Rabalais, 31).

One might therefore contrast Gautreaux's blue-collar characters with those of some of his southern contemporaries, whose darker vision of humanity seems to follow more in the tradition of Harry Crews than of Walker Percy. One might describe the plot of Larry Brown's *Joe,* for example, in terms similar to a typical Gautreaux plot—the title character tries to make up for past mistakes with his own children by being a better role model to young Gary Jones—but in the Brown novel, Joe ultimately introduces the naturally responsible Gary to sex and alcohol, both of which have been sources of his own troubles. Certainly Joe's good intentions and conscience distinguish him from Gary's amoral father, but his more appealing example for the boy may be more corrupting to the young innocent. It is easy to reject a father who would sell a son and prostitute his daughters, not so easy to recognize the tragic flaws in the man who "heroically" kills your sister's rapist. Matthew Guin's description of the "deterministic poverty and social indifference" found in the fiction of Larry Brown, as well as Dorothy Allison and Harry Crews,[26] simply does not apply to Tim Gautreaux. So even as Gautreaux adds to the body of literature being written about the blue-collar class in the South, he reminds us that no group is homogenous.

In tune with his blue-collar characters, Gautreaux knows (and loves) machines (which figure prominently throughout his

UNDERSTANDING
TIM GAUTREAUX

Understanding Contemporary American Literature
Matthew J. Bruccoli, Series Editor

Volumes on

Edward Albee • Sherman Alexie • Nicholson Baker • John Barth
Donald Barthelme • The Beats • Thomas Berger
The Black Mountain Poets • Robert Bly • T. C. Boyle • Raymond Carver
Fred Chappell • Chicano Literature • Contemporary American Drama
Contemporary American Horror Fiction
Contemporary American Literary Theory
Contemporary American Science Fiction, 1926–1970
Contemporary American Science Fiction, 1970–2000
Contemporary Chicana Literature • Robert Coover • Philip K. Dick
James Dickey • E. L. Doctorow • Rita Dove • John Gardner
George Garrett • Tim Gautreaux • John Hawkes • Joseph Heller
Lillian Hellman • Beth Henley • John Irving • Randall Jarrell
Charles Johnson • Adrienne Kennedy • William Kennedy • Jack Kerouac
Jamaica Kincaid • Tony Kushner • Ursula K. Le Guin • Denise Levertov
Bernard Malamud • Bobbie Ann Mason • Cormac McCarthy
Jill McCorkle • Carson McCullers • W. S. Merwin • Arthur Miller
Lorrie Moore • Toni Morrison's Fiction • Vladimir Nabokov
Gloria Naylor • Joyce Carol Oates • Tim O'Brien • Flannery O'Connor
Cynthia Ozick • Walker Percy • Katherine Anne Porter
Richard Powers • Reynolds Price • Annie Proulx
Thomas Pynchon • Theodore Roethke • Philip Roth
May Sarton • Hubert Selby, Jr. • Mary Lee Settle • Neil Simon
Isaac Bashevis Singer • Jane Smiley • Gary Snyder
William Stafford • Anne Tyler • Gerald Vizenor • Kurt Vonnegut
David Foster Wallace • Robert Penn Warren • James Welch
Eudora Welty • Tennessee Williams • August Wilson • Charles Wright

UNDERSTANDING
TIM
GAUTREAUX

Margaret Donovan Bauer

The University of South Carolina Press

© 2010 University of South Carolina

Published by the University of South Carolina Press
Columbia, South Carolina 29208

www.sc.edu/uscpress

Manufactured in the United States of America

19 18 17 16 15 14 13 12 11 10   10 9 8 7 6 5 4 3 2 1

Library of Congress Cataloging-in-Publication Data

Bauer, Margaret Donovan, 1963–
    Understanding Tim Gautreaux / Margaret Donovan Bauer.
        p. cm. — (Understanding contemporary American literature)
    Includes bibliographical references and index.
    ISBN 978-1-57003-859-4 (cloth : alk. paper)
    1. Gautreaux, Tim—Criticism and interpretation. I. Title.
    PS3557.A954Z59 2010
    813'.54—dc22

                                                              2009034327

Tim Gautreaux's stories take me home to Louisiana where I hear the music of the voices, taste the spices of the food, and remember family and friends.

I dedicate this book to fellow aficionados of fine literature who can appreciate this writer's mastery of his craft.

I have no doubt there will be Cajun literature in the future. The area is too fertile and alive with stories, traditions, and legends to remain fallow forever. The Cajun story, however, will not be told by someone from outside the region who has simply a knowledge of literature and writing. The person who tells the Cajun story will have to be a Cajun himself or herself. . . .

Dave Peyton, 1979

Contents

Series Editor's Preface

The volumes of *Understanding Contemporary American Literature* have been planned as guides or companions for students as well as good nonacademic readers. The editor and publisher perceive a need for these volumes because much of the influential contemporary literature makes special demands. Uninitiated readers encounter difficulty in approaching works that depart from the traditional forms and techniques of prose and poetry. Literature relies on conventions, but the conventions keep evolving; new writers form their own conventions—which in time may become familiar. Put simply, *UCAL* provides instruction in how to read certain contemporary writers—identifying and explicating their material, themes, use of language, point of view, structures, symbolism, and responses to experience.

The word *understanding* in the titles was deliberately chosen. Many willing readers lack an adequate understanding of how contemporary literature works; that is, what the author is attempting to express and the means by which it is conveyed. Although the criticism and analysis in the series have been aimed at a level of general accessibility, these introductory volumes are meant to be applied in conjunction with the works they cover. They do not provide a substitute for the works and authors they introduce, but rather prepare the reader for more profitable literary experiences.

M. J. B.

Acknowledgments

I begin my acknowledgments with the subject of this study, Tim Gautreaux, who did not (as any writer might) seem to fear my writing a book on his work. Rather he cooperated from the start, sending first his encouragement and then his latest novel while it was still a Word file, then allowing me to come to visit him and his wife, Winborne, for an interview as well as many hours of talking off the mic during a most enjoyable visit to their western North Carolina home. A note of appreciation also for friends and colleagues near and far who share my enthusiasm for the well-crafted short story and Tim Gautreaux's mastery of the genre, and thanks to the other friends and family who simply support me in whatever I'm working on. At the end of one of his interviews, Tim Gautreaux says, "When the writing's going really well, I figure I'm doing what I was meant to do, and there's no better feeling than that."[1] I heartily agree. This book project was motivated by a particularly frustrating year of academic quixotism that made me appreciate all the more the heroes in Tim's fiction, who step in and do something tangible to make change. Thus a special note of appreciation to the late Matthew J. Bruccoli and the University of South Carolina Press, who said yes to my inquiry about whether it was time for a volume on Tim Gautreaux for the Understanding Contemporary American Literature series.

Understanding Tim Gautreaux was written with the support of a 2008 East Carolina University Faculty Senate Research / Creative Activity grant, which provided a summer stipend and funds for traveling to interview the author and a graduate student stipend to transcribe the interview. I thank ECU English

Department graduate student Elizabeth Howland for her excellent transcription and ECU undergraduates Christina Mahan and Melanie Gnau for their help checking quotes and endnotes during their internships with me. I also appreciate the detailed reader's report from Jerome Klinkowitz, who read this manuscript for the University of South Carolina Press.

Chapter 1 was adapted into an introduction to Tim Gautreaux that appeared with my interview with him, "An Interview with Tim Gautreaux: 'Cartographer of Louisiana Back Roads,'" *Southern Spaces,* May 28, 2009, http://www.southernspaces.org/contents/2009/bauer/1a.htm.

The discussion of "The Piano Tuner" in chapter 4 is adapted from the discussion of this story in my book *William Faulkner's Legacy: "what shadow, what stain, what mark"* (© 2005, used here with the permission of the University Press of Florida).

Acknowledgment is made to the publishers and other copyright holders listed below for permission to quote extensively from Tim Gautreaux's works:

From *Same Place, Same Things* by Tim Gautreaux. Copyright © 1996 by Tim Gautreaux. Used by permission of Picador, an imprint of St. Martin's Press, LLC, and SLL / Sterling Lord Literistic, Inc.

From *The Next Step in the Dance* by Tim Gautreaux. Copyright © 1998 by Tim Gautreaux. Used by permission of Picador, an imprint of St. Martin's Press, LLC, and SLL / Sterling Lord Literistic, Inc.

From *Welding with Children* by Tim Gautreaux. Copyright © 1999 by Tim Gautreaux. Used by permission of Picador, an imprint of St. Martin's Press, LLC, and SLL / Sterling Lord Literistic, Inc.

Introduction

> When I was a kid, somebody gave me a new typewriter
> and I figured I ought to use it. I started to write to pen
> pals from around the country, but very quickly I ran out
> of things to say, so I started to make things up, to lie to
> these people about my life—how I was hunting alligators
> and things like that. It was just fun to tell stories.

In a 1989 article on "The Image of the Cajun in Literature,"
Marcia Gaudet explains,

> Major American writers from Henry Wadsworth
> Longfellow to Ernest Gaines have written about Louisiana
> Cajuns. The images of Cajuns range from the quiet, pas-
> toral view found in Longfellow's *Evangeline*, to the lazy,
> stupid, naïve, happy Cajun of later writers, and, more
> recently, the violent, threatening, racist Cajun. In fact, while
> writers have produced a variety of stereotypical Cajuns that
> range from the totally inaccurate to the somewhat narrow,
> one-dimensional image, there has not yet been an accurate
> portrayal of the Cajun people or their culture by a major
> American literary figure.
>
> Beginning with Longfellow's *Evangeline* (1847), the
> Acadians in Louisiana have usually been portrayed by writ-
> ers who lacked any real knowledge or understanding of the
> people or the culture.[1]

Longfellow, Gaudet notes, "had never been to Louisiana" (86)
and "never pretended his account was based on fact," yet "his

depiction of the Acadians as a simple, pastoral people formed the core for the popular image of Louisiana Acadians in the nineteenth century" (77). In the twentieth century, the image of the Cajun changed. In particular, Cajuns appear as "violent, dangerous, [and] bigoted," usually "from the perspective of the black man" (85). The best-known writer to provide this perspective is Louisiana's Ernest J. Gaines, whose Cajun characters are part of "a segregated society during a time of crisis." Gaudet points out that Gaines "never pretends to be showing the Cajun from the perspective of an 'insider' in the Cajun culture, [for] he never shows the Cajun from the Cajun point of view" (86).[2] As James H. Dormon had already observed in his 1983 book *The People Called Cajuns*, Cajuns "rarely speak for themselves"[3] in the various sources that reference them—historical, biographical, or literary—that is, until Louisiana's Tim Gautreaux began publishing his stories. Gautreaux's name reflects his ethnicity—he is a descendant of the French Acadians who settled in southern Louisiana after the British drove them out of Nova Scotia in the eighteenth century—and in his fiction the reader finds the Cajun perspective written *from* a Cajun perspective.[4]

In spite of Gautreaux's significant role in adding this previously seldom heard voice to southern and American literature, the author resists such labels as "southern writer" or "Cajun writer." And certainly his fiction is not limited to the perspective of Acadian descendants—or even southerners: the two main characters of his second novel, *The Clearing*, are from Pennsylvania. While the main characters of his other two novels, *The Next Step in the Dance* and *The Missing*, are Acadians, the characters in his short stories are more likely to have working-class backgrounds than to be identified as specifically Cajun. His protagonists are predominantly white, blue-collar, south Louisiana men, ranging in age from the twenty-something men of his novels to the numerous grandfathers in his stories. It is the Louisiana white working man's story that Gautreaux tells—or rather the various stories of blue-collar workers, a voice fairly new to southern literature in general, offered by other writers of Gautreaux's generation (such writers as Mississippi's Larry Brown and South Carolina's Dorothy Allison), all countering or deconstructing the poor white and "white trash" stereotypes of their writing predecessors from wealthier and more educated heritages. Echoing Arthur Miller's defense of Willy Loman as an appropriate source of tragedy, Gautreaux defends his focus on "blue-collar subjects" in his fiction when he says, "An uneducated, poor person still has a significant life."[5]

Born on October 19, 1947, in Morgan City, Louisiana, Timothy Martin Gautreaux is the son of a tugboat captain and the grandson of a steamboat chief engineer. Other men in his family worked for the railroad and offshore on oil rigs. Many men in his family enjoyed storytelling, so it is not surprising that Gautreaux wound up a master of the short story genre. He attributes the moral vision of his fiction to growing up in the 1950s:

> Whatever comes out on the page is just who I am. I don't consciously have designs on readers as far as trying to convince them that one thing is right and another wrong. My narratives support what I feel to be true. You know, there's one thing about the old days, the fifties, when everybody believed in two or three things, two or three systems of belief and not unlimited roll your own philosophy—which is what we have today. There was a sense that everybody was on the same page. That's the era I was raised in. You didn't cheat people, you didn't lie, and you didn't hit anybody over the head, unless they deserved it. Also, you

observed the finer rituals. You went to church; you were responsible for your mistakes; you owned up to them. If you did something bad, you didn't blow it off, you felt guilty about it, and tried to make amends. That's something I think a Muslim can relate to, a Jew, a Christian—just that sense of responsibility. I create characters who resemble folks I grew up with, responsible people. I think a lot of readers like that.[6]

Gautreaux's responsible people differ significantly from the anti-heroes of much of contemporary fiction, and his moral vision offers a more optimistic perception of people who will, more often than not, choose to do the right thing. Though somewhat nostalgic for the shared communal values he remembers from the 1950s, Gautreaux is neither sentimental nor idealistic. He is simply not cynical, and he likes the people and places he writes about.

After attending parochial schools for his elementary and secondary education, Gautreaux went to Nicholls State University in Thibodaux, Louisiana, from which he graduated in 1969 with a major in English. One of his professors there entered some poems Gautreaux had written in a Southern Literary Festival contest held in Knoxville, Tennessee. Keynote speaker James Dickey read the winning poems, among them Gautreaux's, and invited Gautreaux into the Ph.D. program at the University of South Carolina, where Dickey was then teaching. Gautreaux's dissertation was a volume of poetry called "Night-Wide River" (1972).

According to Gautreaux these few years living outside of Louisiana while in graduate school taught him "how different Louisiana was, south Louisiana in particular, from the rest of the country . . . the food . . . the religion . . . the politics . . . attitudes," which remind the reader that the South is not monolithic—perhaps a reason to resist, as he does, a label such as "southern writer."[7] In Columbia, South Carolina, Gautreaux's understanding of his own culture really began: "At that point it began to be clear to me what being Cajun was. . . . It had to do with attitudes, the value of food, the value of religion, and things of that nature. And it's sort of an attitude about life. The attitude that though people think they're better than you, you know different" (Hebert-Leiter, 70). Gautreaux's appreciation of his culture and his understanding that sometimes you have to leave a place in order to reach such an appreciation would influence his novel *The Next Step in the Dance*.

After receiving his doctorate, Gautreaux returned to Louisiana in 1972 to teach at Southeastern Louisiana University in Hammond, a town east of Baton Rouge and about sixty miles northwest of New Orleans. His new wife, Winborne Howell, a North Carolina native he had met in graduate school, accompanied him. She had completed a master's degree program at South Carolina and accepted a job teaching at Southeastern. Five years after moving back to Louisiana, Gautreaux applied for a seat in a fiction-writing class taught by Walker Percy at Loyola University in New Orleans. Percy selected Gautreaux in addition to other writers, such as future novelist Valerie Martin and future *Time* magazine managing editor Walter Isaacson, who would go on to have successful careers, and from this experience on, Gautreaux wrote fiction.

With the heavy teaching load of a small state institution, along with raising two sons (Robert and Thomas) and maintaining interests beyond academia (Gautreaux continued to enjoy his various hobbies), it took him a while (well into his forties) to surface on readers' radar,[8] but Percy's apparent recognition of talent was well deserved: after a couple of early publications in small literary magazines, Gautreaux's stories were accepted by such premier venues as the *Atlantic Monthly, Harper's*, and *GQ*, and from these publications they were selected for the anthologies *The Best American Short Stories*,[9] *New Stories from the South: The Year's Best*, and the O. Henry Awards' *Prize Stories*. His stories also attracted the attention of fiction writer Barry Hannah, who invited Gautreaux to be the 1996 John and Renée Grisham Southern Writer-in-Residence at the University of Mississippi, which would give him a respite from his usual teaching load long enough to allow him to finish his first published novel.

Gautreaux's first book, a collection of twelve stories, was published by St. Martin's Press in 1996, just a year before the writer's fiftieth birthday. *Same Place, Same Things* was blurbed by fellow Louisiana writers James Lee Burke, Robert Olen Butler, Andre Dubus, and Shirley Ann Grau and then picked up for review by the *New York Times*. Calling it "a terrific debut collection," *Kirkus Reviews* noted the writer's "sympathetic understanding of working-class sensibilities" and compared Gautreaux to Flannery O'Connor.[10] The Catholic magazine *Commonweal* praised the collection's stories for providing a "welcome relief from the blandness of McWorld; they bring reassuring evidence of the continuing existence of places away from the big place where, increasingly, we all live."[11] And the reviewer for the *North American Review* remarked upon Gautreaux's character development, noting that the author "knows how to get out of a story's way and just let the characters do what they need to do. . . . These characters move through the world compelled by important motive. The characterizations are swift and precise, rooted in gesture, speech and action."[12]

Gautreaux's second book, the novel *The Next Step in the Dance* (Picador, 1998), was also reviewed in the *New York Times*, and the reviewer remarked upon the author's "poetic mix of colorful detail and rapid-paced suspense" as well as "his keen ear for Cajun dialect."[13] Writing for the *Missouri Review,* John Tait also admired Gautreaux's "unmatched ear for the speech of rural Louisiana" as well as his talent for writing about machines: "Here is a writer who can make the refitting of an engine as compelling as another author's love or death scene." This reviewer, however, also found that the novel "suffers from a lack of urgency and momentum" and "overstays its welcome,"[14] not recognizing, it seems, what a Louisiana reviewer understood about the importance of this book: Susan Larson wrote in the *New Orleans Times-Picayune* that the 1980s setting, "a time of great trauma for this state[,] . . . certainly deserved a literary piece to memorialize it." In her review Larson quotes the author, reminding us of Louisiana's "diversity of cultures and values," which inevitably will change as Louisiana becomes part of the McWorld that the reviewer of *Same Place, Same Things* discovered was absent from Gautreaux's stories. But Gautreaux also reassures his readers in his comments to Larson that "Louisiana's not going to stop being a good place to write about. It's going to be hard to exhaust this state because it's so rich,"[15] and certainly with this novel and a collection of stories, he was not finished mining material for fiction.

In 1999 St. Martin's published a second volume of Gautreaux's stories, *Welding with Children*, and the *New York Times Book Review* again picked it up for a lengthy and positive review, praising the author for his "cartograph[y in] mapping with affectionate but unflinching accuracy both the back roads of Louisiana . . . and the distance between parents and children."[16] Reviewing this collection for the *Hudson Review*, Susan Balée calls Gautreaux "the master of the Cajun short story" and one of the three "best short story writers *in America* today"— praise that would certainly please a writer who resists regional labels.[17] And reviewer Alan Heathcock lauded the author's "invention of clever, out of the ordinary conflicts" and "his ability to render true the voice of his Louisiana working-class characters." Heathcock summed up the collection by noting that "the stories are all about people who want to be good, who want to help others and end up helping themselves in the process. They are about redemption, with a tender sense of humor, as seen through the kind eyes of their author."[18]

With three books in print, Gautreaux tackled a historical novel set in the 1920s, after World War I, dealing with a veteran suffering posttraumatic stress disorder, perhaps thus prompting the comparison of his second novel, *The Clearing* (Knopf, 2003), to Charles Frazier's Civil War novel, *Cold Mountain,* in *USA Today*.[19] The *New Yorker* responded to *The Clearing* by calling Gautreaux a "Bayou Conrad,"[20] and several reviewers began to compare (and contrast) the author to Cormac McCarthy. *Publishers Weekly* suggests that *The Clearing* confirms the opinion that "Gautreaux is perhaps the most talented writer to come out of the South in recent years."[21] His growing reputation is reflected in the larger number of reviews of this novel in a broader spectrum of venues, from local papers to the *Christian Science Monitor* and the UK's *Guardian*, as well as in the immediate and broad response to *The Missing*, another post–World War I novel published by Knopf in 2009. For both novels the author certainly did his homework, researching the place and the time for authentic details that would allow him to depict realistically life in the 1920s in a Louisiana lumber mill town in *The Clearing* and on an entertainment steamboat going up and down the Mississippi in *The Missing*. As Alan Warner wrote in his review of *The Missing* for the *Guardian*, "Gautreaux's historical fictions are structured like exquisite machinery."[22] Writing for the *Richmond Times-Dispatch*, Doug Childers noted, too, that *The Missing*'s "anti-war sentiments and arguments for forgiveness over revenge will resonate for many contemporary readers."[23]

Gautreaux may resist being called a southern or Cajun writer—believing as he does that *all* writers are regional writers, that writers just naturally set their work in the region they know best and write about the people around them—but he acknowledges without reservation how Catholicism influences his writing, remarking that "it's impossible to write about South Louisiana culture without writing about the Catholic Church, because it permeates everything" (Masciere, 31). Unlike Flannery O'Connor, to whom he is most often compared by reviewers and the literary critics who are already analyzing his work, Gautreaux is surrounded by fellow Catholics in his native Louisiana, but like O'Connor, his characters are not all Catholic. They do all face some kind of moral dilemma and, reminiscent of O'Connor's stories, often have the opportunity to choose grace, but they are more likely than the typical O'Connor character to accept the grace they are offered. Gautreaux's moral vision is ultimately more optimistic than O'Connor's. He often refers to his former teacher Walker Percy regarding writing about moral issues: "In Percy, I saw a writer who was experiencing his divine gift. His novels deal with moral issues, religious issues. That was very influential on me. . . . I don't see fiction that does not have some kind of moral concern as being very interesting."[24]

Another writer who has apparently influenced Gautreaux is fellow Louisianian Ernest Gaines. Gautreaux has pointed out how "Gaines created his entire fictional universe out of a single gravel lane in Point Coupée Parish" in spite of having left Louisiana as a teenager to live in California for much of his life. From this observation about Gaines's body of work, Gautreaux discerned that "a writer . . . owns a certain literary territory. It's the place of his birth, where he grew up, the language that he listened to, the values that were implied, and the everyday commerce of his life" (Hebert-Leiter, 66–67).

Another characteristic of a writer's literary territory is the point of view. As noted, Gautreaux writes primarily from the south Louisiana working-class man's perspective. A few of his main characters have a little more education, and he has one Catholic priest protagonist (in "Good for the Soul") and one Protestant minister protagonist (in "The Pine Oil Writers Conference"). For the most part in Gautreaux's fiction, women play supporting roles as wives or serve in motivational roles, inspiring the male protagonists to action; occasionally they play the villain or at least are somewhat antagonistic toward the male leads. There are two female protagonists among the short stories' main characters (in "Died and Gone to Vegas" and "Returnings"), and the first novel has two protagonists, a man and a woman.

Surprisingly, in spite of the Deep South setting of Gautreaux's oeuvre, there are very few black characters, and only three who play major roles—the title character of "Deputy Sid's Gift" and the housekeeper, May, and her son, Walter, in *The Clearing*—though the black musicians as a group do play an important role in *The Missing*. Thus, just as Ernest Gaines has written the stories of the African American man of Louisiana (even in his

books) and views writing fiction in mechanical terms: "The thing about a properly designed mechanism is that there are no non-functioning parts. Everything has a purpose, every bit and tag, screw and eyelet. Good fiction's the same way."[27] In the close readings of his individual stories and his novels in the following chapters, the reader will find that Tim Gautreaux's "good fiction" does reflect this theory of writing.

CHAPTER 2

Same Place, Same Things

It's kind of a distilled form of altruism, and there is a
point in many of my stories where the character feels put
upon by fate because he says, "I gotta make this decision:
I can turn around and I can walk away—or I can help."
And when he makes that decision, then the story is
rolling.

When asked which genre he prefers as a writer, Tim Gautreaux
says, "The short story; it's controllable" and "more of an art
form, really, than the novel": "You can work on a short story
sentence by sentence almost the way you work on a poem. And
you can micromanage it. You can go back over it many times
and make everything line up. You can make sure that the logic
of the first sentence ties in with the logic of the very last.
You can't do that with novels; they're just too large." Gautreaux
comments, too, on the importance of the short story: "Think of
the major American writers who are known more for their short
stories than for their novels. That statement goes back to
Hawthorne and Poe and applies to contemporary writers like
Joyce Carol Oates," whose anthologized stories, rather than
their novels, are how they are usually introduced to students
(Bauer, "Interview"). Gautreaux also has remarked upon how
readers have found his work through his stories' appearances in
magazines, which may then draw them to the novels and story
collections when they see his books, along with so many others,
on the shelf of a bookstore.[1]

Several stories in Gautreaux's first collection, *Same Place, Same Things,* not only appeared in primary venues for story publications but also were then selected for regional and national "best" volumes.[2] The collection's title story and "Died and Gone to Vegas" were published in the *Atlantic Monthly,* from which "Same Place, Same Things" was selected for the 1992 volume of *The Best American Short Stories* and "Died and Gone to Vegas" for *New Stories from the South, 1996: The Year's Best.* The founding editor of *New Stories from the South,* Shannon Ravenel, also picked "The Bug Man" after its 1994 appearance in *GQ,* in which Gautreaux also published "Little Frogs in a Ditch," which Annie Proulx selected for *The Best American Short Stories 1997.* And "Waiting for the Evening News," which appeared in the literary magazine *Story*, received the 1995 National Magazine Award for Fiction. *Story* also published "People on the Empty Road," and "Deputy Sid's Gift" appeared in *Harper's.* Gautreaux attributes his jump almost directly into major magazines such as these to being "a perfectionist when it comes to short fiction" and to his maturity as a writer who began publishing his stories in his forties: "It takes twenty years for you to develop the language skills, the intellectual filters in your brain that tell you what to put on the page and what to leave off the page" (Bauer, "Interview"). In interviews he has explained his "method" as "rewriting," describing the numerous "specialized passes" he makes through a story as he revises, "the myopia of [which] helps me really make a story take on a certain type of polish." This kind of attention to craft is reflected in the stories, which are reminiscent of the work of another Louisiana writer, Kate Chopin. Though his stories are much longer than hers, like hers, they have no extraneous material, which Gautreaux says is intentional: "Every line, every sentence has to have some sort of connection to what you're trying to do in the way of theme, in the way of narrative. I like to tell students that a short story is like an automobile engine; there are no redundant parts. . . . Everything in the story has to have some kind of a function. This means that what determines a good story is not so much what's in it but what's not in it. It's important to know what to cut."[3]

"Same Place, Same Things"

> He was poor himself, at least as far as money goes, but he was not hangdog and spiritless like many of the people he'd met in this part of the state, beaten down and ruined inside by hard times. (2)

The pump repairman of the title story of Gautreaux's first collection introduces the author's prototypical protagonist: a blue-collar working man who comes across the proverbial damsel in distress. Unusual for Gautreaux's short stories, which are typically set in contemporary Louisiana, this one is set during the Great Depression. Harry Lintel, a pump repairman in his mid-forties, arrives at a farmhouse in rural Louisiana during a drought and, after receiving directions to the pump from the woman at the house, finds the farmer out in the field, dead, apparently electrocuted while trying to fix the pump on his own. Though discomforted by the woman's unveiled distaste for her husband as she directed Harry to him, the repairman is still hesitant to report back directly to her the news of the farmer's death. Assuming her husband's death would be distressing to her, regardless of the woman's feelings for her husband, he asks where the nearest neighbor lives and sends that woman to break the news to the widow while he finds a phone to call the sheriff.

As Harry then goes about other repair jobs of this day, "saving little farms from turning back to sand" (5), Gautreaux notes his protagonist's particular talent in this role: "The repairs were hard ones that no one else could manage" (5). Harry's sensitivity to the mechanical problems of engines mirrors his intuitive sensitivity about the people around him. Besides recognizing the wife's attitude toward her husband, he noted her isolation on the farm and the apparent fact that she "didn't even have children to take her mind off her loneliness" (6). He also is not deaf to the subtle observations of others that might have warned him to stay away from this woman: when the widow appears the next day in a field near another of Harry's jobs, the farmer with him remarks that "a woman what walk around like that with nothing better to do is thinking up trouble. . . . When a woman thinks too long, look out!" (7). But Harry is a sympathetic man, and though he is troubled, "scared" even (8), by this woman and does not believe he understands what is going on with her beyond the loneliness he detects, he is drawn to her, the way many of Gautreaux's Good Samaritans are drawn to those they find in some kind of need.

The need of this woman is to get away. Looking back at their first conversation, the reader might consider her surprise that "anyone would come to this part of Louisiana from somewheres else," together with how she calls Harry "a traveling man" (3). When she brings him a picnic lunch the day after her husband's death (not caring how this might look to others), Ada (who tells Harry her name in this section of the story) remarks, "Must be nice to take off whenever you've a mind to. I bet you travel all over" (9). Then she seeks Harry out at the local café and asks him about the places he's been, "listening to his tales of mountains as though he were telling her of China or the moon" (10).

When Harry questions her about why she keeps showing up, she responds directly, "Maybe I want to move on" (11). Later she adds, "Sometimes I think it's staying in the same place, doing the same things, day in, day out, that gets me down. Get up in the morning and look out the window and see that same rusty fence. Look out another window and see that same willow tree. Out another and see that field. Same place, same things, all my life." Then, hearing a train whistle, she "looked off toward it" (12–13).

Harry is intrigued by Ada, attracted by her implied willingness to trade sexual favors for a ride out of town, and, a widower himself, he also empathizes with her loneliness. He misses his wife and calls himself "a man who travels" rather than a traveling man (3). The reader discerns that he is a man who would probably prefer the domestic life that Ada feels trapped by, and though Harry's instincts tell him to be wary of this woman, he considers taking her with him, wondering, "Would this heal what was wrong?" (13). Before committing himself to a traveling companion, Harry checks out what is bothering him, stopping at the widow's house when she is not home, where he finds the pump switch inside, still turned on. Of course the farmer would have turned this off before going out to work on the pump. The reader should recall here that Ada mentioned to Harry having seen his ad in the newspaper (3) as well as the neighbor's warning. Realizing that the woman killed her husband deliberately—indeed, may have been inspired to do so upon seeing Harry's ad and then thinking of Harry as a ride out of town—and remembering that this is her third dead husband, Harry "shook like a man who had just missed being in a terrible accident" (14).[4]

Harry successfully avoids the widow after this, and as he continues to work throughout the Louisiana parish, he redirects his mind from thoughts of her to the memory of his deceased wife until a rainstorm arrives and his service is no longer needed in this area. At his first stop to eat on his way to the next drought area, Harry finds Ada hiding in the bed of his truck and gently rebuffs her request to continue traveling with him—interestingly by telling her, "*If I could help you*, I'd bring you along for the ride" (15; emphasis added). Like Christ's priests (Catholicism informing all of Gautreaux's fiction, even stories like this one in which the characters are not specifically Catholic), he can only save those who want to be saved, who express regret and ask for forgiveness. When Ada accuses him of being hardhearted, he tells her more bluntly, "No, ma'am. . . . I loved a good woman once, and I could love another. You can't come with me because you killed your old man" (16).

In his reading of this story, Ed Piacentino seems to agree with Ada's view of Harry: Piacentino calls Harry "self-absorbed and standoffish" and perceives his refusal to help Ada as reflecting some failure on Harry's part rather than Harry resisting the temptation to end his own loneliness because it means helping a woman who has just gotten away with murder.[5] Piacentino's reading does not reflect Gautreaux's tendency to place his characters in the middle of a moral dilemma and then to have them choose the proffered grace (in contrast to many of Flannery O'Connor's characters, who more often reject this opportunity). Harry resists the allure of Ada, but, instead of turning her in to the local authorities, he gives her money for a bus ticket—back home—punishment enough to her, he knows, for her crime. And he was certainly right about her: she takes the money and then knocks him out with a wrench and steals his truck, admitting to him as he falls, "I've never met a man I could put up with for long. . . . I'm glad I got shut of all of mine" (16).

Julie Kane suggests that "Same Place, Same Things" "is the story most reminiscent of O'Connor. . . . Typical of O'Connor . . . are the 1930s Southern rural setting, the attractive traveling 'mystery man,' the sudden turn toward violence, and the hope of grace and transcendence." Kane also lists elements that are still "all Gautreaux's own": "the sharply etched Louisiana landscape, the natural dialogue . . . and the machines that seem to exude the presence and dignity of human characters."[6] One might add that in contrast to the ending of O'Connor's "A Good Man Is Hard to Find," Gautreaux neither leaves his protagonist murdered nor gives the murderer the last word. O'Connor gives the story's final words to the Misfit as he looks down upon the body of the grandmother. At the end of Gautreaux's story there is a suggestion of grace: "Near dusk he woke to a dove [a symbol often used to represent the Holy Spirit] singing on the phone wires" (16). Symbolically resurrected, Harry is not bitter and expresses no anger toward this woman; he maintains his ability to view her situation sympathetically, even as he distinguishes himself from her: "She was a woman who would never get where she wanted to go. He was always where he was going" (17). In these two sentences, L. Lamar Nisly points out, "Gautreaux is able to suggest the kind of rootedness, the sense of who he is, that allows the repairman to be able to right himself after his encounter with this rootless and ruthless woman."[7] Harry neither expresses regret over his lost truck nor wonders regretfully if he will survive, and the reader is left not entirely certain that he will live, for Gautreaux does leave Harry on the side of the road as the story closes: "One eye began to work, and he watched clouds, the broken pieces of the world hanging above like tomorrow's big repair job, waiting" (17). The tone is hopeful; whether Harry is waiting for death or another Good

Samaritan to come to his aid, he is at peace with himself. So
while this story, which introduces and titles the collection, does
not end with a successful rescue and the conversion and reform
of the woman, a failure that recurs in many of the stories of
Same Place, Same Things, the tone is not pessimistic. Gautreaux
has not yet reached the more consistent comedic optimism of the
stories of his next collection, but the spirit of hope is there
already, right from the start of his first book.

"Waiting for the Evening News"

> Hardly forty people knew he existed, and now his name
> had sailed out into the region like parts of his exploded
> train. (23)

On his fiftieth birthday, Jesse McNeil blows up a town. That's
how the evening news tells it, at least. In truth he was merely the
train engineer and the catastrophe is the result of an accident.
But Jesse *was* drunk, and he *did* run away from the scene, and
it is not unusual for people to seek someone to blame when
tragedy ensues. How convenient to have an absent engineer to
point the finger at if you are a "hophead [brakeman who]
smokes weed day and night" (26) or the owner of the train or of
the chemical company that produces the contents of the explod-
ing tanks or a now homeless citizen or a news reporter looking
for a story angle.

Ironically, just before the train inexplicably derails, Jesse was
feeling pretty anonymous, and though "laughing at how free he
felt," he was also thinking "how nobody cared what he was
doing" and "how lost he was in the universe" (20). The reader
realizes that the laughter is sardonic and that the reason Jesse
"wanted to do something wild and woolly, like get half-lit and

pull the chemical train, known by enginemen as the 'rolling bomb,' up to the Mississippi line on time for a change" (19), is that he is feeling as though his life has made no difference and his imagination is so limited by this tedious life that making the route on time while drunk is the only challenge he can come up with for himself.

In short Jesse meant no harm and expected no consequences of drinking on the job. As his wife, Lurleen, describes his life to television reporters, "not one thing that man would do would surprise a jumpy cat" (27). And yet, waking the morning after his flight, Jesse is certainly surprised to find himself on the morning news, considered to be a fugitive from the law. The title of this story alludes to Jesse's belief that his sudden fame will dissipate by the end of the day: "Waiting for the evening news, Jesse pondered life's good points, how most injuries healed up, most people changed for the better, and whatever was big news today was small potatoes on page thirty tomorrow" (25–26). While Jesse had previously felt inconsequential in his anonymity— "The sense of being invisible made Jesse think he could not be taken seriously, which was why he never voted, hardly ever renewed his driver's license, and paid attention in church only once a year at revival time" (25)—he is now feeling encouraged by his usually mundane life, that is, until the evening news brings him pictures of the devastation left behind by the train wreck and the news "that somehow everything was being blamed on him" (26).

Avoiding the idea of his responsibility for any of the ensuing tragedy, Jesse skips the local news the next evening, only to find his wife talking to a CBS reporter on the national news, expressing her lack of surprise over the allegations of her husband's responsibility for the accident. The news story turns from

Lurleen to how ten thousand hens died from a toxic cloud that rolled from the wreck site over a chicken farm and to the firemen who succumbed when the wind shifted; then the announcer comments that Jesse's fellow workers speculated about his depression over turning fifty and his marriage problems, concluding, "Whatever the reasons, he left behind a growing scene of destruction and pollution perhaps unequaled in American railroad history" (28). Insignificant Jesse McNeil, out looking only for a cheap thrill on his half-century birthday, has made history.

While it seems clear that the accident is not Jesse's fault, Gautreaux does explore the recurrent theme of individual responsibility found throughout his work. In this story he focuses on every individual's responsibility in the wake of a tragedy. What is Jesse guilty of? First of all, of running away rather than facing the consequences for drinking on the job. While Jesse may be right that this "catastrophe . . . would have happened even if he had been stone-sober and riding the rails with a Bible in his back pocket," looking back to the moments just after the accident, the reader realizes that Jesse never consciously registers the full significance of what he himself witnessed just before he ran: "The first chemical tanker exploded, pinwheeling up into the night sky, slinging its wheels and coming down into a roadside 7-Eleven, the building disappearing in an unholy orange fireball" (20). Jesse does not consider the clerk(s) and potential customer(s) inside of that building, and juxtaposed against this description is his realization that "the strange pounding Jesse heard was the sound of his own feet running" (20–21). While he was running, someone could have been dying, so though he may not have been responsible for the wreck, he also did not try to save any lives afterward.

Gautreaux is somewhat easy on this weak character; he does not say whether anyone died in the 7-Eleven, nor does he mention the deaths of any people in the story (the firemen who are caught by the shifting wind are "seriously injured" [28] but evidently not killed). The town is destroyed forever, given the toxicity of the chemicals, so consequences are serious, but the author is more concerned with Jesse's soul in this story, it seems, and so he sends to his protagonist a priest, who picks up Jesse as he hitchhikes "south toward the alien swamps and that Sodom of all Sodoms, New Orleans" (21). Thus begins Jesse's soul searching as the priest, who welcomes a companion to keep him awake on the road, engages in conversation about the nature of Jesse's religious background after discovering that Jesse, who has told Father Lambrusco that he is a carpenter, does not know who the carpenter Joseph was. The priest does not try to convert Jesse upon learning of his fundamentalist rather than Catholic background; he merely engages Jesse in conversation about differences between religions, asking if Jesse's baptism was "by total immersion" (22) and whether it changed his life, and the two talk about snake handlers and nuns. But the religious theme of this story goes much deeper than the priest's sympathy for a man he believes is merely down on his luck. The reader is not surprised (nor does it feel too coincidental) when the two men meet up again in Jackson Square during Jesse's period as a fugitive. Gautreaux is gently guiding his protagonist to recognize his *responsibility* even if he is not *guilty*. It is not the carpenter Joseph, surrogate father of Jesus, whom Jesse (only masquerading as a carpenter) might come to relate to; his recent experience can teach him more about Jesus himself, an innocent man who accepted responsibility for the sins of all. Reflecting this association between Jesse and the lesson Jesse might learn from Jesus,

Gautreaux poses his character, first with "outstretched arms" in front of the television screen, asking, "What have I done to you?" and then "framed in the mirror by a spiked crown of hair" (29) after he has gotten a new hairstyle to change his appearance and avoid recognition now that his face keeps appearing on the news.

A week after the accident, Jesse and Father Lambrusco meet up again, and Jesse's spiritual education continues. From the sense of injustice for being blamed for much more than he was responsible for, Jesse must come to recognize that the point is, rather, that he was responsible for himself, and that included not drinking on the job and not running away, as well as paying more attention to the world around him. He sees Lurleen on television more clearly than he has seen her in years and notices that she is still attractive when previously he had focused only on what he considered her menopausal nagging. Also on national television, "he watched his partially bald yard, his house, which from this angle looked like a masonite-covered shoe box, and his carport, which seemed wobbly and anemic under its load of pine straw [and] imagined voices all over America saying, 'Is that the best he could do after fifty years?'" (28). He is embarrassed by the possibility that Lurleen will tell the reporter about how he never paid a relative for painting their house, so he is feeling guilty about something, if not about the train wreck. But regarding the more serious crime he has committed, he begins to wonder "whether he might have noticed something wrong with his train had he been completely sober," from which thought he "looked back over his whole life much as a newscaster would do in a thumbnail sketch, and he shuddered to think that he had been guilty of many mistakes" (31). He calls his wife and is surprised to find that she is worried about his safety, having perceived that the furor over the compounding tragedy has aggravated the public's reaction to her missing husband. Recognizing her concern, Jesse "realized that there might be more to Lurleen than he'd noticed . . . that she had become one of the details of his life that he no longer saw" (32).

With this further awareness of what, if not the train wreck, he *is* guilty of, Jesse meets with Father Lambrusco a third time, over lunch, which significantly the priest buys for the man (a communion feast of a sort). Over this meal Jesse confesses his "sin" (simply, who he is or rather *that* he is—as we are all—a sinner) and asks what he can do. Though not a Catholic who knows the routine of the confessional, he naturally seeks a penance, but the priest responds that "it can't be undone. Just turn yourself in. Ask forgiveness." As in the previous story, the point is that he can be saved only if he expresses regret for the act. Jesse ponders the priest's words: "Forgiveness from whom? he thought. The railroad? The crossroads town? The millions and millions who followed his mistake on television?" Now he feels like Judas and wonders if Judas understood how he would go down in infamy, but still he gives the priest permission to turn him in "about news time" that evening (33). Thus, unlike Peter, he does not deny Jesus during this third questioning.

Jesse goes back to the hotel and reads Genesis "for some clue to how everybody's troubles began," understanding, it seems, the idea of original sin, the natural sinfulness of mankind, which his baptism did not wash away since he has refused to really see himself before. When the police and a SWAT team and a helicopter and a news camera show up at the hotel that evening, Jesse (drunk again) opens the door to them all shouting, "Everybody knows who I am or what happened" (34). Now he compares himself to Noah, another drinking man and yet "the one they let run the ark. . . . The Lord trusted him to save our bacon." Even God's chosen ones have been guilty, Jesse realizes. He is ashamed now of the drunk he sees on the television set behind him, even has he turns to face the crowd. The person standing there and the person on the screen, he tells the police officer who comes up to arrest him, "feel like . . . two different people," suggesting, too, that he recognizes himself as both that drunk who may have caused the train wreck and "as empty-handed and innocent as every man on earth" (35). One is again reminded of an O'Connor story ending—Mr. Shiftlet outrunning the mushroom-shaped cloud threatening a storm in "The Life You Save May Be Your Own." But in contrast, Gautreaux's story *began* with the character trying to outrun the wrath of God. In its concluding line, Gautreaux's protagonist is "bathed by strobes and headlights and stares, locked in inescapable beams" (36), prepared to take responsibility and face his punishment for being a sinful human being.

"Died and Gone to Vegas"

> "Okay, Nick, you the only one ain't told a lie yet. Let's have some good bullshit." (51)

"Died and Gone to Vegas" might be viewed as the first of the handful of stories in which Gautreaux inserts a character from his academic world among the more typical blue-collar Louisianians found throughout his work. Mark Twain–like, these stories often take a somewhat mocking tone toward a sometimes condescending educated character, the audience for the vernacular storyteller. These stories therefore reflect what Julie Kane calls the "double-consciousness" of Gautreaux's blue-collar heritage and his Ph.D. in literature.[8] In spite of his own college degrees, Gautreaux has noted his preference for the language of the "uneducated," considering standard English "not conducive to storytelling," as he told Christina Masciere: "There is still a rich creative metaphorical magic alive, and it's in the mouths of uneducated people [who] have to make up an idiom as they go along" and thus are "acrobatic with the way they use the language."[9] So for stories such as "Died and Gone to Vegas," Gautreaux evidently drew from many years of "listen[ing] to retired tug-boat captains and oil-field workers try to outdo each other in stories" (Bolick and Watta), and the success of this particular story, at the center of which is just such a storytelling situation, is due to his ability to capture the different storytelling voices he has enjoyed and admired.

"Died and Gone to Vegas" opens with Raynelle Bullfinch, a cook on a dredge boat, telling Nick, "the young oiler" working to earn money for college, that "the only sense of mystery in her life was provided by a deck of cards." She contrasts her own dead-end job with Nick's temporary employment on the boat, saying, "Nick, you're just a college boy laying out a bit until you get money to go back to school, but for me, this is it" (37). Similar to Jesse McNeil's limited imagination, Raynelle's fantasy life, limited by her experiences, extends only to winning enough money playing cards for a trip to Las Vegas, where she can play with a higher class of people.

Gautreaux acknowledges "elements of the old tall tale and frontier humor in [his] writing," explaining, "Much of my early reading was devoted to folklore and the likes of Mark Twain" (Bolick and Watta). In the tradition of southwestern humorists, as the characters in this story play cards they strive to outdo each other with tall (and taller) tales.[10] As the pot of money grows in the center of the table, so too does Raynelle seem to expand with a suppressed but building anger, perhaps at the misogynistic tone of some of the stories. She demands to know "what happened to that poor girl" (50) as one story comes to a close—and the teller, recalling how "Raynelle had permanently disabled a boiler-maker on the *St. Genevieve* with a corn-bread skillet" (50–51), adds an ending in which the fat wife mocked in the story diets and slims down, though another worker then adds, "That's the scary thing about women. . . . Marryin' 'em is just like cuttin' the steel bands on a bale of cotton. First thing you know, you've got a roomful of woman" (51). In spite of the misogynistic depictions of women in the stories, it is more likely the predictability of the storytelling that is truly bothering Raynelle, for men do not come off much better in the tales than women; they are victimized and made fools of just as often. The stories reflect the various prejudices of the card players, but none of the listeners seems much offended as long as the story entertains. Clearly what these people are doing is fending off boredom.

One would be as hard pressed to find a moral in these characters' tall tales as in those told by the vernacular narrator of Mark Twain's "The Celebrated Jumping Frog of Calaveras County." The point is the storytelling itself, and everyone must participate, even the college boy. At the beginning of the story, Nick had pled ignorance of the card game they are playing, and toward its end he is expressing a similar reluctance to participate in the storytelling. But everyone must pull his and her weight on this boat, and that includes helping to break the monotony of the job. Just as Raynelle had told Nick the simple rules of *bourrée*, a Cajun poker game, and mocked him for his hesitation about playing—"This ain't too hard for you, is it? Ain't college stuff more complicated than this?" (38)—so too does she taunt him when he claims not to know any good stories: "A man without bullshit. Check his drawers, Simoneaux, see he ain't Nancy instead of Nicky." Goaded, Nick begins a tale, and Raynelle prompts him along with a question about the name Nick gives his character, Gonzales. "Was that his first name or second name?" she asks. "Well, both," he tells her, thus giving his story its first element of incredibility. And then he seasons the tale with stereotypes not unlike those peppering the stories of the other tellers: "You know how those Mexicans are with their names. This guy's name was Gonzales Gonzales, with a bunch of names in between" (51). In contrast to the others, however, Nick's story has a recurring theme beyond its incredibility. Repeatedly Nick notes that this Gonzales "knew who he was" (53), and it is his certainty of self that saves his life when a drunk threatens to shoot him for lying about his name and where he lives (on Gonzales Street in Gonzales, Louisiana): Gonzales gestures for a phonebook and the bartender looks him up for the man with the gun. Again in comparison with most of the other stories told, Nick's story allows the character to make good, claiming he is the G. Gonzales of a local car dealership. Everyone is impressed. Nick becomes one of them just as Raynelle wins the pot of money that has piled up during the storytelling.

This Gautreaux story "has been referred to as a Cajun *Canterbury Tales*," which Gautreaux finds apt. "These people all want to go on some kind of pilgrimage [to] the secular shrine of Las Vegas," he says.[11] With winnings beyond her dreams (about $650), Raynelle again expresses her fantasy of going to Las Vegas, and when the pilot asks if she'll bring one of them with her, saying, "We all want to go to Las Vegas," she repeats her wish to "gamble with gentlemen" (54–55). Nick is still caught up in the storytelling mood of the evening. He starts imagining Raynelle in Vegas, wearing her silver lamé dress but standing out among the "tourists dressed in shorts and sneakers" (55) rather than fitting in with the gentlemen gamblers of her fantasy. But Nick is also the character Gautreaux refers to as not exactly the author himself but the closest he comes to putting himself into stories, the "little guy who has kind of a straight vision of the truth and sees through the imagined realities of the storytellers" (Kane, "Postmodern," 130). The story closes with Nick's imaginative vision, in which he projects a dismal future for Raynelle not unlike the fates of the characters in the stories told around the card table. The long-haired oiler just earning some money for college may be the only one at the table likely to escape the monotony of the others' jobs. That does not make him superior to his fellow workers; rather it pressures him not to allow his own life to become mundane. Perhaps like the others he will continue to tell stories, but he will write them down, sympathetically capturing the culture of his native Louisiana in all its variety for readers beyond the world of the boat.

"The Courtship of Merlin LeBlanc"

> He couldn't raise her. What if he died? Worse, what if he didn't do any better with her than he had with his own? (66)

With this story Gautreaux introduces the first of many grandfathers in his fiction who find themselves suddenly responsible for their grandchildren. These men are of a generation for whom it was not unusual for the woman to provide the primary care for the children while the men were out working, although since Gautreaux usually writes about blue-collar families, one should note that the women generally work outside the home, too. The focus in these stories, though, is not on the dual roles of the working mothers but on the singular role of the male protagonists, which resulted in their disengagement from their children. As these men observe their adult children, they are puzzled by the lack of shared values evident in the children's lifestyles. In "The Courtship of Merlin LeBlanc," for example, the title character's daughter has two failed marriages and an illegitimate baby, and the impetus for the crisis that prompts the events of this story is her decision to fly off to Mexico for a weekend with someone she just met. Merlin agrees to babysit for his granddaughter even though he disapproves of his daughter's plans, and he is awakened during the night by a phone call telling him the plane has gone down in the gulf.

Merlin takes this news quite calmly in spite of the fact that this is the third of his three children to die and that he is a widower. He is not in shock; he is just unresponsive. We hear from both his father and his grandfather later in the story that this coldness is not unusual for him. But as is typical in Gautreaux's worldview, it is never too late to change, and the death of his last child, along with suddenly being faced with the responsibility for her child, seems to prompt some self-examination: "The loss of his first two children had saddened him, but he had denied or concealed the sorrow in his life. Now he sensed an unavoidable change coming, as though he were being drafted by the army at his advanced age" (58). Merlin has already, by the time he receives the phone call, "realized with a pang that he couldn't keep his eyes off [the baby] for a minute" (57). After receiving the news of the plane crash, "he looked at the blond head on the blanket, and a powerful fear overcame him. What would he do with her?" (58).

Gautreaux backs up at this point as Merlin recalls his last meeting with his daughter, when she brought the baby to him.

Their interaction reveals that each is aware of the other's lives, even as they are clearly not close. Merlin can tell that Lucy has been crying, and she knows that he has just finished his harvest and thus is available to babysit. He also knows that there would be an "and" in her story as she sets up her problem for him: she is "going nuts hanging around Ponchatoula doing nothing" *and* she has a plan to do something about her dilemma, for which she needs something from him. He observes her appearance as he approaches her "across the close-clipped St. Augustine." Her "dirty-blond hair was pulled back into a limp ponytail, and her eyes were baggy and pained. They were looking at him but they had a faraway quality he had seen before *and never tried to understand*" (59; emphasis added). The reader might note the contrast between Merlin's apparently well-groomed lawn and not-so-well-put-together daughter. While he has "never tried to understand" his daughter, he does pay attention to his property. Though he does not approve of the trip she is planning, he opts for not having to "hear about yet another deadbeat she was going out with" and agrees to take care of Susie in order to cut off Lucy's story. The narrator notes that "though he was tempted to tell her she was making a mistake, he held his tongue, as he always had with his children. He was a man who never offered his children advice yet always marveled at how stupidly they behaved" (60).

In these stories about generational differences, Gautreaux's older characters are often puzzled by their children's different values. Why do the children not share their parents' work ethic and morality? they wonder. Why are the children not more successful than their parents, as would be expected in the natural order of things? Indeed Merlin's children do not even outlive their parents, and their unnatural deaths (besides Lucy's death in a plane crash, one son dies in a drunk-driving accident and the other is shot during a poker game) reflect the unregenerative environment of the LeBlanc household even as the fields outside are apparently quite fertile. The reader learns in this story little about Merlin's wife except that she was hard working, both on the farm and in the kitchen, "honest and a good cook." But as Merlin ponders the idea of finding another wife to help him take care of Susie, he realizes "he couldn't remember how he'd felt the day he'd married, couldn't remember one thing he had said to his wife. After all those years of marriage he hadn't known much about her" (65). Merlin's cold detachment, which his father and grandfather both attest to being a characteristic trait ever since he was a child, may have served him well as a farmer, but it has also contributed to his (almost) empty house. In his usual tendency toward sympathizing with his imperfect characters and offering them an O'Connor-like moment of grace, Gautreaux gives Merlin a second chance with this granddaughter.

Concern about leaving this child in the hands of his hard-hearted son at first prompts Merlin's father to recommend that his son find a wife—hence the story's title. As frustrated with his son as Merlin was with Lucy, Etienne does, in contrast to his son, respond to Merlin's reaction to this suggestion—"I could use someone to cook and clean up"—with "I'm not talking about a cleanin' lady. . . . You got to find someone you can care about," but then he notes, "Aw hell . . . I forgot who I was talking to" (62), so he doesn't press. But the reader subsequently learns that this is how Merlin may have gone wrong. Etienne never expressed his disapproval of Merlin's behavior, thus establishing the pattern that Merlin would then follow with his own children. Merlin is not the only character facing his mistakes in this story; both father and son are contemplating their role as father in their children's lives.

After a couple of weeks as primary caregiver of the baby, Merlin realizes how much work raising a child is, "thought of his dead wife and was ashamed of himself." He is painfully reminded again of how exhausting his late wife's life had been when he dresses up to go out to find a replacement wife to take care of this baby, "dug around in the medicine cabinet for something to make himself smell good . . . found a green bottle with no label and slapped on some of its contents" only to realize after feeling it burning his skin that the bottle contained "a foot liniment his wife had bought" (62). After this first unsuccessful night looking for a potential wife in a bar, Merlin also realizes that, at his age, wives will come with grown children "who would soon be after him for hand tools and car-insurance payments" and that they might not be that interested in a small child: one woman points out to him that she is past "that yellin' and stinkin' stage. I already done my time" (64). It is interesting that this story, which begins with the death of a young woman, is among Gautreaux's most humorous. He is not failing to take her tragedy seriously; rather, as in "Waiting for the Evening News," he focuses on the character for whom there is still hope, Merlin, a pretty unlikable guy, it seems, so that comedy rather than sympathy draws the reader in to his story.

Starting a new family is not the answer for Merlin LeBlanc. The answer, his grandfather ultimately shows him, is courting the family he already has, Susan (not Susie, the old man insists, which sounds like someone he would pick up in that bar), "talk[ing] to her every day about everything. Tell[ing] her about dogs and salesmen. . . . About cooking [her grandmother] and cars and poker [her uncles] and airplanes [her mother]" (71). Susan can be the first generation of this family to learn lessons from the previous generations while she is young, with her whole life before her. But the two old men are also learning from each other and from Octave, Etienne's father and Merlin's grand-father. As he berates Merlin, Etienne recognizes his own failure to live up to the example his father had set: "'We all married young. We didn't know no more about raising children than a goat knows about flying. He knew,' Etienne said, straightening up and touching his father's shoulder. . . . 'When I saw how you was ignoring your kids, I should have come and whipped your ass good three or four times and thrown you in the slop with the pigs. . . . He told me to do it, too'" (70). The old patriarch in the wheelchair, slipping in and out of consciousness recently, as though dying and rising from the dead is part of the natural order of things, had apparently not spared his son his opinion in order to avoid hearing more than he wanted to know: "Merlin feared his [grandfather's] directness, didn't understand it. But he was ninety-three years old and all his children were still alive." He asks his grandfather for mercy—"Don't be hard on me, Grandpop"—and the answer he is given, "Somebody shoulda" (67), accuses both of the other men. The story closes with these men standing in the sunshine—like Jesse McNeil caught in the spotlight—"chastened but determined" (71) and in awe of the smiling baby and old man, both with so much to teach them.

"Navigators of Thought"

> Bert noticed that they had buckled their life vests correctly
> for once. They had no time to think about what they were
> doing. (83)

From the student earning money on a dredger to go back to college in "Died and Gone to Vegas" to a tugboat full of unemployed college professors in "Navigators of Thought," Gautreaux pokes fun at the more educated of his characters even as he shows them the same sympathy that he has for his more typical (i.e., less educated) blue-collar workers. On board the significantly named *Phoenix III* are five men who couldn't make it in academia but are clearly also not suited for the work they've found, except perhaps for Bertram Davenport, the captain of this crew of misfits, who is actually not unhappy in his new vocation. The others are just earning a living until they find publishers for their manuscripts, which will help them to get back in front of a classroom.

Bert found his way into this line of work first. Taking a ferry to pick up his unemployment checks, he discovered that "he liked the gritty smell of the Mississippi" and was impressed by the tugboats and freighters: "The throbbing vessels moved with the power and grace of great poems." After a year of having no luck finding another academic job, he decided "to apply to a towing company for work" and was hired, largely because Dixon, a less educated man who owned the company, wanted to teach the college professor a lesson. It was a surprise to them both, but Bert got along fine with the other workers, who Dixon "was sure [would] throw him overboard first trip out," and "became an excellent harbor wheelman, learning the currents and signals as though they were in his blood" (77).

Like Mark Twain, Bert is torn between his natural inclination toward river piloting and his supposedly higher cultural ambitions, and he finds his "success" on the river bittersweet in that it "told him that he was a better river man than he had been a teacher. When he recalled how he had often bored his students and become disoriented while dealing with complex ideas in his lectures, he suspected that the English department was right in getting rid of him" (77). A man who knows himself and whose view of the world around him is pretty clear (if a bit flowery; the similes abound in this story as Gautreaux thus comically captures the perspective of a somewhat out-of-place poetic mindset), Bert shares his new world with others who did not make it in his old world: "Max, his old graduate school roommate, an amiable but directionless man who worked on car engines for extra money and who had earned his final degree at forty-one after taking dozens of diverse and ill-chosen courses and then writing a seven-hundred-page dissertation on Byron and Nietzsche"; "Dr. Laurence Grieg, who had been fired two years before for failing too many students, and whose hobby was preparing French cuisine"; Thomas Mann Hartford, an interesting name for an English professor; and Claude McDonald, "a man who was a true academic, very intelligent, but so educated that he was unable to compose two coherent paragraphs in a row" (77–78). In spite of Bert's talent, the crew is so inept that Dixon gives them an old tugboat they can't possibly destroy (or so he thinks).

While Dixon "could appreciate the true value of intellectuals," the narrator remarks with heavy irony, he does understand what it is like to feel out of place. In contrast to this crew of failures, Dixon was apparently so successful in his original work (he started where these men end up) that he now owns the business, but "the former deckhand still looked out of place in his fine office, his gray suit." So even as he mocks this ridiculous crew, remarking after one of their accidents, "Please don't try to explain nothin' . . . I wouldn't understand what you was talking about if you did" (75), he does not fire them. And perhaps his choice of the supposedly indestructible *Phoenix III* is his attempt to help them start over, even if he does not recognize the relation between its name and his good intentions.

One of Gautreaux's funniest stories as one reads it—owing to Dixon's ironic mockery of his crew, the men's ridiculous failures, the overly poetic metaphors within the narrative that reflect the disjunction between the men and their milieu—"Navigators of Thought" has a surprisingly tragic ending (in contrast to the humorous "Courtship of Merlin LeBlanc," which began tragically). When the *Phoenix III* is capsized by a runaway barge that the men, surprisingly, were able to lasso, Max goes down with it, trying to save the only copy of his dissertation. Though the men are usually supportive of each other during their critiquing sessions out on the river as they waited for tow calls, when they realize that Max is willing to risk his life for his manuscript they candidly tell him, "It's not worth it. . . . It'll never be published" and "Give it up. It's a piece of crap." But Max is apparently the most desperate to get back into academia, and he goes back for the already soaked pages in spite of his friends'—and probably his own—awareness of the manuscript's chances of becoming a book. Max is ultimately right in believing the manuscript "will get [him] out of here" (84), for he dies going after it.

Arriving on the scene to help with the rescue, Dixon is genuinely upset to find only four men and asks immediately and specifically for the missing crewman. The others respond ambiguously, protecting their comrade by not saying how he got trapped in the engine room. Indeed they seem less distraught over their lost friend and colleague than Dixon is over the simple idea of a lost man. They recognize that Max committed suicide; Dixon would not understand why one would kill himself over a stack of typed pages. Both responses are equally legitimate in Gautreaux's nonjudgmental worldview. Like the river, which, as Bert observes at story's end, "renew[s] itself every flowing moment without a thought" (85), Gautreaux does not ask us to overthink this story (as these "Navigators of Thought" might have, before these events); we should just let these men be, as they (the four left, that is) are now finally at the point of just letting themselves be.

"People on the Empty Road"

> He used his recklessness like a tool to get the job done.
> After every twelve-hour day, he would tear out of the gravel
> pit in his rusty Thunderbird, spinning his wheels in a dimin-
> ishing shriek for half a mile. (89)

Readers leave the four "Navigators of Thought" staring
resignedly at the river and then meet Wesley McBride, who is at
the end of a rope whose significance he cannot grasp. We are
introduced to Wesley, appropriately, in the middle of a fight with
his girlfriend. The two are sitting in a car, and in his frustration
Wesley "crushe[s] the accelerator, leaving the car in neutral, letting the racket do his talking" (87) until there is an explosion
from underneath the hood. The engine activity is an analogy for
Wesley's problem; he cannot articulate what is troubling him—
to himself or to others—and he is on the verge of some kind of
explosion because of this difficulty.

Battling over Wesley's soul are his father, who cares about
him and tries to draw him toward a job that requires patience
rather than one that thrives on his impatient nature (he wants
Wesley to come to work for him as a butcher, so that Wesley
would have to slow down or risk losing *another* piece of finger),
and Wesley's current employer, the owner of the gravel company
who appreciates Wesley's fast driving since time is money for
him. Though Wesley does not know what it is exactly that
makes him so impatient, he does know that his behavior is haz-
ardous to his health; but every day he continues to work as a
truck driver, he breaks his own delivery (and speed) record. One
morning Wesley's attention is caught by the soft, seemingly
unflappable voice of the host on a radio talk show. No matter
how ignorant or rude her callers are, she maintains both her

composure and her patience. Later that same day, while on a gravel run during which he "again chose to see the windshield as a big video-game screen he could roar through with the inconsequence of a raft of electrons sliding up the face of a vacuum tube" (93), Wesley has a near collision with a school bus. After his boss gets him out of jail, Wesley—shaken by the idea that he could have killed children—goes in search of Janie Wiggins, the radio announcer, to find out "how [she's] so patient with people" (95). Janie's initial response, claiming she "was born patient," is not encouraging, but she also listens patiently to Wesley, until, that is, he expresses his desperation: "It's just that I've been sort of waiting for things to turn around in my life. Right now, I got the feeling I can't wait any longer." This remark breaks through Janie's composure, and she tells Wesley that her "favorite uncle used to say something close to that, over and over. Nobody knew what he really meant until we found him on his patio with a bullet in his temple" (96). So though Wesley has clearly upset Janie, she does seem to recognize the seriousness of his problem and decides to help him.

They begin by going for a drive in her uncle's old Checker, which, Janie notes, this other apparently impatient man found "relaxing to drive, and one of the only things that brought comfort to his life" (97). She lets Wesley drive and observes the reflections of his impatience in his behavior: "You rode the bumper on two elderly drivers . . . signaled for dimmers from two cars who had their low beams on . . . six jackrabbit starts, and at the traffic light you blew your horn. . . . That woman was looking in her purse and would have noticed the light in a second. And where were *you* going? To a summit meeting?" (97–98). Observant of the signs of Wesley's impatience, Janie makes no claim to be able to change him; indeed she tells him she does not know what is wrong with him and says simply, "Just be patient. . . . You have to wait for things to turn around" (98). But she shows up the next day for another driving lesson, during which she has Wesley pull out behind a cattle truck so that he will "realize that if you can wait out this, you can wait out anything" and, more important, learn the lesson he should have learned from his concern about the children huddling in ditches and under the school bus, just waiting to see if he was going to run over them: "A road is not by itself, Wesley, even if it's empty. It's part of the people who live on it, just like a vein is part of a body. Your trouble is you think only about the road and not what might come onto it" (99).

The lessons continue. Janie has Wesley wax her car, slowly, until every spot shines and then read a short story in a magazine and talk about it with her for an hour. They also talk about themselves, "Wesley about his father trying to control his life and Janie about her uncle, how he had raised her, how he had left her alone" (101). But Wesley still has difficulty seeing past the windshield. Now perceiving every experience with Janie as some kind of test of his patience (just as every gravel delivery had been a chance to beat his previous record), when a drunk in a bar begins to make a nuisance of himself, Wesley sits back to prove he can control his temper, merely asking the man once to leave Janie alone but then doing nothing when Janie is dragged onto the dance floor. Here again, then, Janie reveals the crack in her armor. She tells Wesley, just before storming out, "I felt abandoned" (103), and the reader, if not yet Wesley, realizes that underneath her calm exterior, Janie is still devastated by her uncle's death. Not unlike Wesley, this uncle failed to think about the other people on the road, particularly his niece, whom he left alone when he put a gun to his head.

Janie disappears from town and from Wesley's life after losing her patience with a caller on the radio, but she has had an impact. Wesley does quit his job, goes back to work for his father, and continues to listen for Janie on the radio as the story comes to a close, perhaps ready now to understand what goes on underneath the exterior of someone else, able to communicate with words rather than by revving an engine. In his more negative reading of this story's ending, Ed Piacentino suggests that Wesley "*resigns himself* to working for his father as a meat cutter, a lackluster, dead-end job, offering the young man little hope for renewal" (Piacentino, "Second Chances," 121; emphasis added). But in Gautreaux's fiction, jobs such as this are not portrayed as signs of failure; Gautreaux's blue-collar workers are among his most positive characters. Settling into a job as a butcher, which will require Wesley to slow down or risk wounding himself, is a positive change from being hired by his previous employer for his reckless willingness to drive as fast as he can, thus endangering himself and others, including innocent schoolchildren. This story, therefore, does not reflect Piacentino's view of many of this collection's characters as "being in a rut, of being unable to break out of their stagnant, dead-end existences." Wesley is *not* one of Gautreaux's characters who "fail to take advantage of opportunities to reconstruct their misshapen lives" (Piacentino, "Second Chances," 132); indeed very few characters in this book fail to change as a result of the experience around which their stories develop. Wesley's development might therefore be more appropriately applied to illustrate L. Lamar Nisly's perception of Gautreaux's vision as ultimately more optimistic than O'Connor's: "Rather than O'Connor's prophetic model of using her characters to make a point with her readers, Gautreaux tends to be kinder to his characters, treating them with respect and allowing them to change within the course of a story."[12]

"The Bug Man"

> He sprayed his way through the homes of the parish, getting the bugs out of the lives of people who paid him no more attention than they would a housefly. (114)

Reflecting again the positive depiction of blue-collar workers in Gautreaux's fiction, as L. Lamar Nisly has observed, a typical Gautreaux story has at its center "an unlikely person serving as a help, even an agent of grace, to someone in need. At times there are service people—a piano tuner, an exterminator—who come into people's homes and end up offering more than what was requested" (Nisly, "Tim Gautreaux's 'Resistance,'" 139). Perhaps Gautreaux's most sympathetic "service" protagonist is called Mr. Robichaux by his politer customers, Felix by his wife, and just "the Bug Man" by others. Felix Robichaux is one of the author's typical Good Samaritans (like the pump repairman in the book's title story). As are the other manifestations of this character type, the Bug Man is a blue-collar worker with a compassionate heart who comes across a damsel in distress and tries to help her. Like later manifestations of the type, he is happily married, so his offer has no ulterior motive—at first.

Felix brings home to his wife the stories of the various people on his route. He has names for each of them so that she can follow the stories of their lives, which his clients either tell him or he witnesses as he moves freely through their houses, reflecting both his trustworthy nature and his invisibility as a mere serviceman who periodically enters their field of vision. He tells about the sad Beauty Queen, a widow still grieving for her husband several years after his death, and about the Slugs, three generations who live in a house so filthy that "the entire house would have to be immersed in a tank of Spectracide to get rid of the many insects crawling . . . around." Mrs. Malone, the widow, often invites Felix to sit down for a cup of coffee; "Father Slug" welcomes him in with the complaint that "the sons of bitches come back a week after you sprayed last time" (112). But neither is self-aware enough to recognize that their current dissatisfaction is largely their own doing. Mrs. Malone greets Felix with "You know me. Up's the same as down" (109); and she's right, he does know her. She just doesn't know herself well enough to realize what she does have as she mourns what she has lost. Felix notices hanging in the den of the Slugs' house the father and grandfather's high school diplomas and thinks, "The tragedy of the Scalsons was that they didn't have to be what they were. The grandfather and father held decent jobs in the oil fields." Also, he notices Mrs. Scalson outside "burning a pile of dirty disposable diapers" (112). When these dirty diapers are first mentioned, the reader just sees them as another detail of these people's unsanitary lifestyle, but after this last stop of the day, Felix heads home, and we learn as the narrator turns to Felix's own domestic setting that what troubles him and his wife is their inability to have children.

The widow in need in this story is much more sympathetic than the femme fatale of "Same Place, Same Things." Felix is moved by her sadness and loneliness, her willingness to sit down and have a cup of coffee with the Bug Man, so when a single lawyer moves into the neighborhood, the exterminator takes on the role of matchmaker. The Beauty Queen and the lawyer do make a striking couple at first, but the story does not have a happy ending for anyone. When Mrs. Malone gets pregnant, the

lawyer breaks off the relationship, and Mrs. Malone, more depressed than before, takes her pain out on the very person who
tried to help her.

During the setup of his story, Gautreaux writes of Felix
Robichaux, "The Bug Man lived in the modern world, where, he
knew, most people were isolated and uncomfortable around
those not exactly like themselves. He also believed that there was
a reason people like Mrs. Malone opened the doors in their lives
just a crack by telling him things. He was a religious man, so
everything had a purpose, even though he had no idea what. The
Beauty Queen's movements and words were signals to him, road
signs pointing to his future" (111). While on some level Felix is
aware that people use him to vent about their troubles, seeing
only someone they can talk to who does not move around in the
same circles they do, Felix does not always recognize his invisibility as a person to these people, even with the daily reminders
of how little attention people pay him: "Most customers let him
wander unaccompanied in and out of every room in the house,
through every attic and basement, as though he had no eyes. He
had seen filthy sinks and cheesy bathrooms, teenagers shooting
drugs, had sprayed around drunken grandfathers passed out on
the floor, had once bumbled in on an old woman and a young
boy having sex. They had looked at him as though he were a dog
that had wandered into the room. He was the Bug Man. He was
not after them" (111). And yet the narrator describes him as
"seeing into private lives like the eye of God, invisible and judging" (118)—and he does judge. Felix is not idealized in this story,
even though he is ultimately the most sympathetic character. He
judges—and he is judged. He cannot, for example, understand
how someone with so many clothes and such a fine home could
be so unhappy while he and Clarisse manage to keep a stiff

upper lip about their sad childlessness. The reader recognizes in Felix's comeuppance that each one's grief is his or her own and is as valid as another's.

Felix and Clarisse have "tried for all their married life, ten years, had gone to doctors as far away as Houston, and still their extra bedrooms stayed empty, their nights free of the fretful, harmless sobs of infants" (113). Their home life seems defined by what (or who) is absent. Felix even "thought the shrubs looked like circles of children gossiping at recess" (112–13). They "lived like a couple whose children had grown and moved out" and "felt accused by the absence of children, by their idleness in the afternoons, when they felt they should be tending to homework or helping at play." Even their car "felt vacant when they drove through the countryside on idle weekends" (113). Clarisse works as a teacher's aid, surrounding herself with children during the day, while Felix wanders through the lives of his clients, unconsciously noting why they don't seem to have the right to their sadness by comparison to his empty life, not realizing that his relationship with Clarisse is something many of his clients would envy. Even (or perhaps especially) "Mother Slug" would recognize the value of a husband who helps his wife clear the dishes and clean the kitchen after supper.

When Mrs. Malone reports to Felix that she is pregnant and her relationship with the lawyer over, Felix thinks he has discovered what his own relationship with her has meant—he will be rewarded for his patience and time listening to her sadness all these years, his efforts on her behalf to bring at least a period of relief to her isolation, with, finally, a baby for him and Clarisse. So, not recognizing the depth of Mrs. Malone's grief over this latest disappointment, he offers himself and Clarisse as parents for this unwanted baby. And even though she dismisses him without an answer, "for the next month he made his rounds with a secretive lightness of spirit, not telling Clarisse anything, though it was hard in the evenings not to explain why he held her hand with a more ardent claim, why he would suddenly spring up and walk to the edge of the porch to look in the yard for something, maybe a good place to put a swing set" (121).

When Felix arrives the next month, Mrs. Malone is clearly cold and dismissive, and when he brings up the subject of the baby, she tells him she has scheduled an abortion for the next day. Desperate, Felix persists, significantly while on his knees spraying underneath her bed: "You, a beauty-contest winner, and him, a good-looking lawyer. What a baby that would make" (121). But her response to that is the cruel implication that the child would be better off never born than with parents like him and Clarisse. "Mr. Robichaux, what would you do with such a baby? It wouldn't be like you and Clarisse. It would look nothing like you," she says looking down at the kneeling man, adding, "It would be cruel to give this child to you. Why can't you see that?" Felix wonders "if she had planned a long time to say what she had said"; perhaps her speech is an act of revenge for having given her hope by setting her up with the lawyer in the first place. Willfully or not, with these harsh words and by telling him of the impending abortion, Mrs. Malone shows Felix the depth of the darkness of her world, which he had previously not really appreciated, and "he reflected on the meanness of the world and how for the first time he was unable to deal with it." He leaves Mrs. Malone "feeling his good nature bleed away until he was as hollow as a termite-eaten beam" (122) when he arrived at the Scalsons', where he finds the Slugs fighting over their dinner. Disgusted with his view of the depravity of humanity that day, Felix loses his composure and starts spraying his bug poison onto the whole family.

Since such an episode inevitably made the newspaper, Mrs. Malone has the perfect excuse to fire the witness to her own "crime," and Felix does not see her again. Somehow he not only stays out of jail but also expands his business to include additional bug men and a receptionist and then the clients of another exterminator who retires. Clarisse gets a teaching degree and continues to surround herself with children in her work, if not at home. One day, when one of his sprayers calls in sick, Felix notices an address on the man's route and decides to make the appointment himself—to Mrs. Malone's house, where the door is opened by a boy who, ironically, won't let him in because "Joe's the one takes care of that for us" and his mother has "told me not to let in anyone I don't know." Felix tries to convince the boy, "You don't have to be afraid of me. . . . I'm the Bug Man," but the boy responds simply, "Not to me you aren't" (125). Like his mother, this boy can see the serviceman so often invisible to others, can recognize when another is not the regular guy, and can distinguish one serviceman from another,[13] all of which reminds the reader that the cruel words of Mrs. Malone were most likely spoken out of her disappointment in the lawyer and her anger at Felix for introducing them. She was, on most days, a sad woman who was able to appreciate Felix's kind spirit. And perhaps Felix's desperation for a child helped her to decide not to terminate her pregnancy; with this child she is probably no longer as lonely, so Felix was, after all, successful in bringing comfort to her, if not to himself and Clarisse. The story is among Gautreaux's most melancholy; he refuses to take it where the reader might like to see it go: babies for Felix and Clarisse. But Felix's business success and Clarisse's career in education suggest that while they may not have gotten what they asked for, the gods do seem to be sending fortune their way for their role in bringing to another what they already had at home—someone to love.

"Little Frogs in a Ditch"

> Lenny blinked twice, perhaps trying to figure out what she wanted to hear. The grandfather knew that she paid for their dates when the boy was out of work. She bought his cigarettes and concert tickets and let him hang around her house when something good was on cable. Often she looked at him the way she studied whatever gadget was whirling in her lathe, maybe wondering if he would come out all right. (144)

Mr. Fontenot is another of Gautreaux's grandfather characters who finds himself raising his grandson, Lenny. In this story the grandson is actually grown, but since Lenny's parents have moved away and Lenny is only sporadically employed, Mr. Fontenot has taken him in. Since this story does not connect Lenny's behavior to anything specific about how he was raised or how his parents were raised, Mr. Fontenot does not, like Merlin LeBlanc, seem to be facing responsibility for Lenny's lax values. Whether Mr. Fontenot had a role in Lenny's character development, he tries, throughout the story, to help Lenny see how his behavior hurts people, including ultimately himself. Lenny's parents have left him, and toward the story's close, so does his good-hearted girlfriend, who gave Lenny every chance to find a conscience underneath his cynical exterior.

The story opens just after Lenny has been fired from yet another job, and the narrator notes that in contrast "the old man

. . . had held only one job in his life, and that one lasting forty-three years." Lenny is angered by the idea of being fired by someone who "didn't have half the brains I got" and moves from commenting upon this to remarking on how many "dumb" people there are in the world (127) and a diatribe against marketing and the gullible people who are convinced by advertising that they need more than, for example, a plain "white four-door car, no chrome, no gold package, no nothing." His grandfather's challenge to Lenny's cynical take on capitalism and the older man's suggestion that "if you work on your attitude a little bit, you could keep a job" (128), prompts what follows in the story. Lenny determines that he will show his grandfather that he can sell anything and, looking around for a far-fetched enough example to prove his point, he decides upon a pigeon. He will sell ordinary pigeons he snatches from underneath the eaves of their carport by advertising them as homing pigeons.

In his remarks for *The Best American Short Stories 1997*, Gautreaux says that this story was inspired by a man calling into a radio show to brag about selling pigeons: "I began to wonder what type of person would sell these birds to folks who would waste fourteen days of their lives following the bogus training instructions. What would it be like to put up with such a person in my family or to have him as a friend? To find out, I put together Lenny Fontenot and had him lose his job. A character needs something out of the ordinary to happen to set him in motion."[14] One might think here of Jesse McNeil of "Waiting for the Evening News," whose soul searching comes after the train derailment, but in "Little Frogs in a Ditch," Lenny Fontenot rejects the moral lesson his grandfather is trying to show him, and by this story's end the reader realizes that it is more Lenny's grandfather's story than Lenny's own. Gautreaux "wondered what would it be like" to have Lenny in one's family. What lessons can someone learn from Lenny while Lenny resists learning from his own experience?

The reader of Gautreaux's later fiction may note description in this story similar to that which Gautreaux would employ in "Welding with Children" (the title story of the next collection) to point accusingly at the grandfather's failure to teach his children self-respect: "At the rear of the lot was a broad, unused carport, swaybacked over useless household junk: window fans, a broken lawn mower, and a wheelbarrow with a flat tire" (129). In the later story Gautreaux would connect the junk in the grandfather's yard directly to how his children turned out (all three daughters wind up with illegitimate children). In this earlier story, in contrast, there is no accusing implication in Gautreaux's description of the unkempt property that there is a connection between the grandfather's values and Lenny's failure. We learn, rather, that Lenny had grown up in "an air-conditioned brick rancher" with parents who are "hardworking types who tried to make him middle-class and respectable" (130), and these are the people who deserted Lenny, selling the house right out from under their no longer juvenile (but still) delinquent. Furthermore, the narrator notes in this story, the reason Mr. Fontenot "had never owned a dependable automobile" was that he "had always driven junk to save money for his kids and grandkids" (129–30). So Lenny's behavior seems merely a rebellion against his parents' middle-class lifestyle and the monotony he perceives in his grandfather's even less affluent surroundings.

Lenny is resentful, too, of the waste he perceives around him—people throwing away money on luxuries like "a riding mower or a red motorbike" (132)—while he has to bum cigarettes from his girlfriend, who also pays for their dates. Besides the reader's recognition that Lenny is actually not really opposed to luxuries so much as he is angry that he cannot afford any himself, his girlfriend also points out to him that having luxuries is one of the things that distinguishes people from animals: Annie concludes her interesting synopsis of *King Lear* by telling Lenny that the source of Lear's anger at how his daughters were treating him (sending away the friends he parties with because he didn't "really *need* 'em") was that "if he only had the things he needed, he'd be like a possum or a cow" and asking, "When's the last time you saw a possum on a red motorbike?" (132–33). Annie's take on the capitalism Lenny condemns is that "owning things is what makes people different from armadillos. . . . And the stuff we buy, even if it's one of your pigeons, sometimes is like a little tag telling folks who we are" (133). The grandfather's message, to complete this lesson for Lenny, would be that what we sell also tells folks who we are, and he is disturbed that his grandson is a shyster.

But Lenny has already advertised his homing pigeons, and soon after this discussion another surrogate father appears on the scene to buy one for his young charge, his nephew, whose mother has left him. The man feels himself "too old to play ball with a kid" so is looking for something else "to keep him busy" (134), and with no evident prick to his conscience, Lenny sells him a bird and then shows him a farcical training regimen that will make the bird familiar with its new home so that they can then take him to a park, let him go, and wait for him to fly home. "He might even beat you there," Lenny says (135). Mr. Fontenot and Annie are surprised but not amused by Lenny's first sale, and Mr. Fontenot is further appalled when Lenny sells another pigeon to an African immigrant, among others. "What's wrong with you?" he finally asks his grandson. Lenny protests against his grandfather calling him "a crook," telling him, "It's all how you look at it," but Mr. Fontenot responds, "There's only one way to look at it, damn it. The right way," and kicks him out after noting candidly, "Your parents got rid of you and now I know why. . . . And it was time they did. They shoved you out the house and got you lookin' for a job, you greasy weasel" (137).

Here Gautreaux inserts his ability to treat sympathetically even the most unlikable of his characters. The reader can finally squirm on Lenny's behalf when he asserts pathetically in defense against this truth telling, "Gramps, they didn't get rid of me. They moved out west," and then pleads, "You can't put me on the street" (137), but we are also not too upset that Mr. Fontenot does not change his mind. Lenny tries Annie's house, but her father remarks that it would not look right, and when Lenny tries to defend his behavior to this man—"I didn't see no harm in it"—Annie's father explains to Lenny, "That's what got him hot. . . . You didn't see no harm in screwing those people. . . . The trouble with you is, you ain't seeing the harm. You see what you want to see, but you ain't seeing the harm" (139). So Annie tries to show Lenny the harm; she has seen poor Mr. LeJeune, the man trying to entertain his nephew, crawling around his property line with the pigeon, and she takes Lenny and his grandfather to witness the pathetic spectacle, where they also realize that the little boy is crippled (and thus the generosity of Mr. LeJeune's nature in not mentioning that perhaps playing ball wasn't an option for the child either). These are *nice* people, and Lenny has taken advantage of them. And what harm has Lenny caused? When the Fontenots and Annie stop to talk with the man and his nephew, they learn that they have trained their bird through inclement weather that has resulted in both having to go to the doctor and "shots in the legs" for the man (143).

When Lenny still refuses to face himself, Annie loses hope. Mr. LeJeune shows up at their house later that night, after they have released the bird in the park, to express his concern about its not having returned yet, and Lenny's failure to refund the money and tell the truth is the end for Annie, who says, like Lenny's grandfather, "Now I know why your parents left your ass in the street." And to Lenny's repeated defense against this accusation, "They're on vacation, you cow," she notes, "People on vacation don't sell their houses, leave the time zone, and never write or call. They left because they found out what it took me a long time to just now realize. . . . That there's a big piece of you missing that'll never turn up" (146). Lenny literally hits back at this emotional jab, but Annie does not take his abuse, and before Mr. Fontenot can reach the kitchen after the sound of Lenny's slap, he hears "a sound like a piano tipping over . . . and Lenny cried out in deep pain" (146). The reader cheers for Annie.

The story takes an interesting turn once the reader realizes that, although Lenny may be pained by the idea of his parents' abandoning him, he does not seem redeemable. When earlier in the story his grandfather told him he needed to go to confession and he asked what he was "supposed to tell the priest," his grandfather reminded him of what he'd learned in his catechism class: "If you close your eyes before you go to confession, your sins will make a noise. . . . They'll cry out like little frogs in a ditch at sundown." Lenny merely responded, "Well, I don't hear nothing. . . . What's the point of me confessing if I don't hear nothing?" (140–41). Mr. Fontenot and now Annie seem to give up on Lenny after he fails to confess to Mr. LeJeune, but as Lenny's grandfather, Mr. Fontenot feels a responsibility to make things right, so he grabs a pigeon that night and heads over to the LeJeune house. Mr. LeJeune catches him trying to replace the missing pigeon and, in a surprising twist, admits that he recognized the con all along. Ironically his nephew's mother also abandoned her son, but unlike Lenny's seemingly decent parents, she is a crackhead, and the boy, Alvin, never knew his father. While Lenny might be irredeemable, it isn't too late for Alvin, Mr. LeJeune realizes, so he has gone through this whole charade to "teach him to deal with the big thing"—his mother's abandonment—by starting with a less heartbreaking disappointment. The boy still believes his mother will be back, "but he's got to toughen up and face facts," Mr. LeJeune says, and revealing the character that will help Alvin to do so without becoming too tough, he adds, "He's crippled, but he's strong and he's smart" (148), a boy to be envied by the grandfather of Lenny Fontenot. Mr. Fontenot would prefer to see the face he can imagine on the boy "if he could see that the bird had returned to the cage" (149), but the reader, along with Mr. Fontenot, recognizes that Mr. LeJeune's way is probably better for the boy. The ending may offer no hope for Lenny, but the reader feels assured that young Alvin will be all right.

"License to Steal"

> I know there's been some gaps when I ain't worked much,
> but you can't work too steady if you're a Louisiana man.
> You got to lay off and smell the roses a bit, drink a little
> beer and put some wear on your truck. (155)

Ed Piacentino suggests that the main character in "License to Steal" may be Gautreaux's idea of how Lenny Fontenot of the preceding story turned out: "Of essentially the same mold as Lenny Fontenot, fifty-two-year-old Curtis Lado in 'License to Steal' represents the kind of character that an older Lenny would likely become if he does not change" (Piacentino, "Second Chances," 122). Habitually out of work, Curtis wakes up one morning and finds neither coffee brewing nor breakfast cooking but a note from his wife declaring, "I had enough." Apparently surprised, he calls his son to find out if she told him anything more. *Not* surprised himself, Nookey responds, "Naw, nothing she ain't been saying since I was born. Said she was tired of living in Louisiana with somebody didn't bring home no money. Said she wanted to move to the United States" (151). Atypical of Gautreaux, this story associates the deadbeat behavior of the central character with a critical attitude toward Louisiana's "Laissez les bons temps rouler" motto. In interviews Gautreaux remarks upon (though not negatively) his own lack of ambition, which he attributes to his Louisiana heritage (Masciere, 47; Kane, "Postmodern," 137). Perhaps it is this attitude that Gautreaux can relate to in Curtis that allows him to treat somewhat sympathetically this one of very few seemingly irredeemable characters in his fiction.

Dissatisfied with Nookey's response, Curtis plans to consult his other son, and when he asks about Buzzy's whereabouts and is informed that he's in jail, he simply asks, "Which one?" (152) and then dials the memorized number of the jailhouse. This son, a drug addict, cannot help his father either, so Curtis figures he had better start looking for work before the power company comes to take his meter and the finance company his television. The personnel employee at the first place he stops is out, so while he waits for her to return, Curtis drives down to a local bar to have lunch—and four beers. Later, with beer on his breath to top off his unconsciously outrageous responses to the woman's interview questions, Curtis, to no one's surprise, does not get the job, but the interview does offer the reader more insight into why

Mrs. Lado left. When asked why he hasn't worked for a number of years, Curtis does not give the response he seems to believe himself and perhaps has used on his family and friends—that "he had a weak heart and that work gave him a nervousness in his chest parts" (152). Believing that the woman might be hesitant about hiring someone with a heart problem, he responds instead (apparently not perceiving that this response might also not impress a potential employer), "You see, my wife had this wonderful job that supported us to just the upmost, and I never was a greedy man. No, ma'am, I figured to work on the every now and then and enjoy one day at a time. My daddy used to say to me, 'Let the future take care of itself and never give a nail two licks when one'll make it hold'" (154). Reflecting this same attitude, the next day Curtis is offended by another potential employer, who expects him to work on Saturdays: "A job like that will run a man into the ground. Six days a week? When the hell will I have time for any recreation?" And when Nookey, who is with him this day of job searching, mentions that he occasionally works on Saturdays, Curtis responds, "Then you got the brain of a armadillo. What you think you're gonna do, get rich? This is Louisiana, son. Ain't nobody can get rich in this state through hard work" (159).

Here again the reader finds the story jabbing at Louisiana, but of course, one must consider the source—in the first instance, the wife of this loser, and in this second case, the loser himself, seeking an excuse for his own behavior, someone to blame for his failures. Though one of the Lado sons is in jail, Nookey does seem to be a decent man; he comes to check on his father the day after his mother's departure, takes his father job hunting, and tries to talk to his father after Curtis insults the first person who seems willing to offer him a job. Besides noting that

working Saturdays is not so unusual, Nookey also calls attention to his father's heavy drinking, but Curtis only responds,
"You want to kill yourself working, go ahead." As Curtis's
response becomes a diatribe, the reader can hear echoes of Lenny
Fontenot of the previous story: "You'll wear your fingers off
down at the weenie plant all your life for what? So you can buy
some trashy piece of red dirt with a used trailer on it while some
real estate fool gets most all your money and a lawyer gets the
rest. You think *they* work hard? You think just because they
went to parties and chased women at a college for four years
that they sweat and worry every day that the sun comes up? Hell
no, son. They don't have a education. They got a license to steal"
(159). The source of Curtis's bitterness isn't identified; Gautreaux does not give any telling background on this character.
But this story's placement right after "Little Frogs in a Ditch"
could suggest that there might not be any more reason in Curtis's past for his cynicism and his shiftlessness than there is for
Nookey, raised by such a father, to have the more admirable
work ethic he exhibits in this story. Gautreaux provides a vivid
portrait of Curtis Lado but does not offer an explanation for
him. Are such people always explicable?

Like Lenny's grandfather, Curtis's son gives up on his irredeemable kin, lashing out as he jumps out of the truck after his
drunk father hits him for trying to take the wheel, "Go on and
drive in a ditch if you want to. I believe Momma was right when
she took off" (160). His remarks remind the reader of Mr.
Fontenot and Annie pointing out to Lenny that his parents left
him. Unmoved by his grown son being near tears, Curtis drives
off to another potential job, this one reminding him of a job
he once had and actually liked. Again there is an opportunity
here, for they actually "need a carriage man to run that old-time

system until we get a new one set up," but the owner of the saw-mill sizes Curtis up right away and dismisses him with "I don't hire old drunks" (161).

On his way out Curtis sees the big saw's carriage and climbs up into it—for old times' sake or to show them what he can do, who knows—starts playing with the lever, and before he knows it he has crashed into and squashed the owner's Cadillac. He leaves in the middle of the man's ranting about suing him and seeing him in jail, and, to compound his troubles, his car won't start, so he just curls up in there, listening to the public radio announcer (with his "educated voice" [163]) introducing an opera by recounting the story of the early French settlers in Louisiana. The story ends with Curtis "listen[ing] . . . carefully, but [the words] were being spoken in a tongue he had not been taught," followed by an "incomprehensible music" (164). Curtis's inability to comprehend what the man is saying reminds the reader that Curtis had earlier bragged to the personnel woman about his eighth-grade education—"further than anybody in my family" (153)—and his pride in Nookey for figuring out he could "quit school in ninth grade . . . and then take a dinky lit-tle test" (154) for his GED (which Curtis puts in the same cate-gory as a bachelor's or master's degree, in response to one of the questions he is asked about his education). So in addition to con-trasting with Gautreaux's more typical praise for Louisiana cul-ture and more usual tone of affection toward his native state, this story also contrasts with those stories in which the author pokes fun at his academic world. In "License to Steal" it is the *un*educated he criticizes, showing the consequences of his home state's failure to value education. There are several comic ele-ments in the story, but ultimately its main character is pathetic— and one of the few characters who tries even his creator's patience.

"Floyd's Girl"

> Can she get turtle sauce piquante in Lubbock? And T-Jean's
> grandmère thought of the gumbos Lizette would be missing,
> the okra soul, the crawfish body. How could she live with-
> out the things that belong on the tongue like Communion
> on Sunday? Living without her food would be like losing
> God, her unique meal. (169)

Balancing the harsh criticism of one aspect of Louisiana's culture
in the previous story, the tone of "Floyd's Girl" toward the
Cajun community that rallies to help Floyd get his daughter back
from his ex-wife's Texas boyfriend is completely positive: "There
was nothing wrong with West Texas, but there was something
wrong with a child living there who doesn't belong, who will be
haunted for the rest of her days by memories of the ample laps
of aunts, daily thunderheads rolling above flat parishes of rice
and cane, the musical rattle of French, her prayers, the head-
turning squawk of her uncle's accordion, the scrape and complaint of her father's fiddle as he serenades the backyard on
weekends." Gautreaux concludes this homage to Louisiana calling these elements "vibrations of the soul" (170), and in this
story he celebrates the family ties; the Cajun food, music, and
speech; the Catholic religion; and the good character of the
Louisiana people at its center. They are no more educated, most
likely, than the Lados, but they do value the intelligence of
Floyd's young daughter.

The crisis that sets this story's fast-moving pace is the kidnapping of Floyd's daughter by her mother's boyfriend, who
plans to take her back with him to Texas, a state so big that
Floyd is unlikely to be able to find her. While the large and violent Texan is the story's obvious villain (he even hits the child to
stop her from screaming), Floyd's absent wife is also villainized

throughout the story—the one, an outsider who has come in and disrupted the order of things; the other, worse, an insider who does not appreciate that order. In spite of her desertion, Floyd considers the woman "still his wife, because once the priest married you, you were married forever, in spite of a spiritless divorce court and a Protestant judge and a Texas lounge bum in snakeskin boots." But it appears that Floyd and his daughter are better off without this woman, for he also notes as he worries about Lizette that she "was scared of her mother, who had beaten her with a damn chinaball branch for playing with her makeup" (167). Lizette's mother is considered "a LeBlanc gone bad," and the description that follows reflects her rejection of the values at the center of this culture: "A woman who got up at ten o'clock and watched TV until time to cook supper. Who learned to drink beer and smoke dope, though both made her throw up the few things she ate. Who gave up French music and rock and roll for country. Who, two years ago, began to stay out all night like a cat with a hot butt, coming in after [Floyd] left for work on Tante Sidonie's farm" (170–71). The various narrative perspectives of the story, including those told from Floyd's view (each section is third-person limited, told from the point of view of the character whose name appears at the start of the section),[15] ultimately characterize Floyd in the opposite terms. He is clearly a man who does appreciate his culture (the paragraph quoted previously enumerating the values of Louisiana is in one of Floyd's sections); he is a hard worker and an honest and forgiving man who would "always do a thing right when it counted" (167).

Contrasting with depictions of Cajuns in popular culture, these people are clearly a peaceful lot, and when the Texan comes in and snatches the little girl right out of an old woman's care, there is little resistance. What could the woman do but send word to the father and then give Floyd directions for catching up with the green truck. Also not much of a fighter, Floyd is quickly knocked down by the Texan when the two meet. But he doesn't give up; he finds one of his uncles, a pilot, and they fly toward Texas and overtake the getaway truck once again, landing a plane on the highway and thus causing quite a spectacle for the next encounter between father and kidnapper.

This section is narrated under the heading "Ensemble," and the witnesses there observe Floyd take another bad beating (along with his uncle). But then the old woman guardian, who has caught up with the truck by this time, notices the child's bleeding lip and steps into the fight—and she does hit a man who is down (Floyd, it had been observed, does not), or rather, she puts a leg of her walker right into his eye. While he is down this time, in pain himself, rather than just resting from the beating he had given, she tries to educate him about the people he is messing with, people who cleared the land they are all on and who have lived here for generations—this is where Lizette belongs, she tries to tell him. But his response is that he'll just come back another time for the girl, so she takes another tactic. Turning to two men in the "Ensemble," the Larousse twins Victor and Vincent (who will reappear in *The Next Step in the Dance*), she asks "if they were still bad boys over in Tiger Island," a challenge to their reputation that they live up to, as the two men take blow torches out of their truck and proceed to disassemble the Texan's truck. When he protests and starts yelling for the police, Floyd asks, "You gonna tell a policeman you stole a little girl that was given me by a judge? You gonna tell him you punched her?" (179). So as Floyd takes his daughter back in the old woman's car, his uncle gives the Texan a parachute and offers to take him home in the plane—and then flies him to the Texas line, where the rescue party also drives to watch the Texan float down from the plane.

"Returnings"

> They refused to reminisce, but they talked around their son at mealtime, as though he were at the table and they were ignoring him. When they touched in any way, the message of him was on their skin, and they knew their loss. Talking could not encompass what had gone from them. (184)

One of Gautreaux's only stories with a woman protagonist, *the* only short story told predominantly from the female character's point of view (though still in third person), "Returnings" is also one of the few short stories set in an earlier time than its writing, though not so far back as "Same Place, Same Things." This story takes place in 1967, during the Vietnam War era. The place is still rural Louisiana, where the main character, Elaine, and her husband (not named in this story, which is her story) own a farm—Elaine doing most of the work at this time, since her husband has hurt his back. Elaine is out in the field trying to restart the tractor, annoyed with herself for having carelessly not taken the time to get the water out of the gas tank after it had been allowed to sit too long. But Elaine at least knows what she is doing, and her mistake is not an uncommon one.

The source of tension in this story is the couple's mourning over their recently deceased son. His death from encephalitis was so unexpected that he remains a ghost between them as they continue on with their own lives. In an era when losing a son in a war would not be so unexpected, they are reeling from the unnatural death of an eighteen year old "who was healthy one week, plowing and fixing things, and dead the next" (184).

"Like most women," the narrator tells us before mentioning the dead son, Elaine "liked to grow things." Elaine herself believes that her "nurtur[ing]" nature and her "drive for generation" make a woman a better farmer than a man with his "mechanical ability." She can "bring life to the fields of her farm," perceiving a connection "between caring for a home and children and raising millions of soybeans" (183). She is not, therefore, discouraged by a tractor not starting, but when the reader soon learns of the lost son, we realize that behind her sense of empowerment over her ability to give life is bafflement over the inability to have sustained it.

Mercifully Elaine is given the opportunity in the course of this story to save another mother's son when a young Vietnamese man brings his helicopter down in the field next to where she'd been plowing (also mercifully, he does not land where she's already passed and thus does not undo any of her hard work). Reading this story as among the more positive in the collection, Ed Piacentino describes Le Ton as Elaine's "newfound surrogate son whom she can guide and nurture, albeit only temporarily, to fill the void left by the death of her own biological son" (Piacentino, "Second Chances," 126). Far from his own family's farm in Vietnam, Le Ton is training at a local military base, and his instructor has given him bad directions in an effort to sabotage his chances of finding his way back. Gautreaux here touches on a xenophobia that shows how the changing South means new prejudices to be explored. The young man explains that if he fails this test, he will end up an infantryman—and as such his chances of dying will increase significantly; he tells Elaine of his own cousin, who died after being kicked out of the U.S. Air Force and into the infantry. Elaine is touched by the threat to this young life (his youth emphasized to her by his smallness), so she suggests going up in the helicopter with him to try to help him find the base. It is interesting that she cannot just give him directions; as we find out later, she forgets about the still-new interstate she might have directed him to, which he could then have followed to the base. The reader is reminded how isolated these rural families are at this earlier, less mobile time, and this is further illustrated when Elaine has Le Ton bring the helicopter down again so that she might ask another farm woman for directions and that woman does not recognize the place names Elaine mentions to try to figure out where they are.

When Elaine realizes she needs to ask for directions, she looks for a clothesline behind the houses below her, which will indicate that a woman lives in the house. In this way she finds another mother, and this one the mother of another soldier whose life is threatened by this war—indeed, as a black man, likely to be sent into the more dangerous arenas. The two women, the one who has already lost a son, the other who could very easily lose hers, help Le Ton, thus perhaps sparing some third, unknown mother the pain of losing a child. For them, unlike the instructor back at the base, the young man's race is not an issue—as their own different races are not an issue as they connect with "a long mother's look . . . the expression a woman owns at night when she sits up listening to a child cough and rattle, knowing there is nothing she can do but act out of her best feelings." The black woman directs the "Chinaman," as she calls him, to the base, familiar with it for having visited her son there, and assures Elaine she will not say anything to anyone, even her son; thus the two women conspire to save this "young [man] laden with possibilities" (191).

Grateful for this help, Le Ton flies Elaine home before following the other woman's directions back to the base. The sound of the helicopter apparently wakes Elaine's husband from a nap (though he doesn't see his wife climb out of it), and when he notices that Elaine has still not restarted the tractor, he goes out to see if he can help her. Keeping her pact with Le Ton and Mary Bankston, the black farm woman, Elaine does not tell what she has been up to but lets her husband think she has been trying to start the tractor all along, even though when he looks to see what is wrong and finds she hasn't yet reopened the gas line, it makes her look more careless. It is then, however, that he admits to having done this himself once, an anecdote that ends with their son asking him, "Daddy, what would you ever do without me?" What, indeed, the couple has been wondering since the boy's death. And with this melancholy thought, they decide to put work aside for a bit and go out. "You need it," Elaine's husband says, and the reader smiles when he adds, "You never get off this place" (193). As they prepare to go out, the phone rings; it is a message from Le Ton letting Elaine know he made it back okay, which she, motherlike, has asked him to do, and he, a good son, has done to put her mind at ease. Gautreaux then brings the story to a close with an image of the future when "the land around [Elaine] would bear cornstalks growing like children." Looking over her field is comforting to this grieving mother, who recognizes that at least for a time, her farm sits "under a safe and empty sky" (194).

"Deputy Sid's Gift"

> Everybody's got something they got to talk about sometime in their life. (195)

Gautreaux closes his first collection with a story told in the first person, the only story not in third person in the whole collection.

Like many of the protagonists that preceded him, the narrator of this story will ultimately accept responsibility, and the reader follows along inside his head as he progresses toward this recognition of his responsibility as a human being to his fellow man. An interesting twist to the first-person perspective, the narrator is a step beyond his initial telling—he is telling the reader about telling a priest of his experience with an indigent alcoholic—and thus is two steps past the story's action. Apparently he is still trying to figure out what it all meant—means—in his life. Also like many of Gautreaux's other protagonists, he is not directly responsible for this other person's hardships, but he *feels* responsible, and he is trying to understand why because he (rightly) suspects that the connection will help him to understand what the experience has taught him about himself and his place in the world.

The time period is apparently the 1980s, when many oilfield workers suddenly found themselves unemployed (thus anticipating the setting of Gautreaux's first novel). Bobby Simoneaux, the narrator of this story, is now working in a nursing home for the elderly, where a priest recognizes from his missing finger that he is out of place "and invited me to come visit at the rectory if I ever needed to" (195). The priest intuited correctly, it seems, for Bobby does seek him out to tell the story of how an old truck he only used for hauling trash to the dump was stolen (and restolen) by a homeless black man; how he found the truck and called the sheriff's office, even though by that time he had replaced it; of his interactions with Deputy Sid, who was with him when they discovered that Fernest Bezue, a local alcoholic indigent, was living in it and who tried to talk Bobby out of taking the truck back or pressing charges (Bobby does agree not to pursue prosecution); and of how he ultimately gave Fernest the truck in an effort to help this man who could not help himself. During his narration Bobby notes repeatedly that the priest avoids eye contact, apparently understanding (as evidenced by "his little purple confession rag hanging on his neck") that "he was hearing my confession" (196). But what exactly is the narrator confessing? Even he does not know.

The title of the story alludes to the person who will help him find the answer—not the priest but Deputy Sid, who, throughout the story, tries to stop the narrator from his pursuit of so-called justice. Bobby admits himself from the start that the stolen truck was so "ratty [that] I was ashamed to drive it unless I was going to the dump" (195), and in fact he doesn't even notice it missing until he goes out one day to use it. He cannot get much response from the police, who tell him they have "more expensive stuff to worry about," so he calls the sheriff, "and when I told them the truck's over thirty years old, they acted like I'm asking them to look for a stole newspaper or something." Here Bobby asserts, "It was my truck and I wanted it back" (196), and it is at this point that he first stops the story to remind us that he is reporting his earlier recounting of events to the priest (with the previously mentioned recognition that the priest, while moving about fixing them coffee, is also behaving as he would when hearing a confession).

Bobby picks up his story recalling how he replaced the truck, "need[ing] something for hauling" (196), and then one day, as he is giving a ride home to one of the nursing home visitors, Bobby's daughter, who is with him that day, spots the truck in some woods off the road. The man riding with them helps to identify the man in the truck but then, when Bobby remarks that he will see that the thief goes to jail, "looked at me with those silver eyes of his in a way that gave me *les frissons*" (197).

Deputy Sid arrives on the story's scene, and he responds similarly. Unlike the narrator, these men perceive right away the pitiful circumstances they are witnessing and are both surprised by Bobby's failure to see past a stolen vehicle to the dire situation of this human being.

When Bobby introduces Sid Touchard into his story, he calls the deputy "that black devil" and describes "his shaggy curls full of pomade falling down his collar, the tape deck in his cruiser playing zydeco." After these details suggesting racial prejudice on the narrator's part, Bobby continues with his negative point of view toward the deputy: "He got out [of the car] with a clipboard, like he knows how to write, and put on his cowboy hat" (197). Although southern literature is often defined by its focus on racial issues, Gautreaux has noted that this story "is as close as I can come to dealing with [race]" in his fiction: "The whole business of racism is very painful to write about" (Levasseur and Rabalais, 33).[16] And indeed, when one thinks over his oeuvre, this is one of very few works in which racism plays a significant role, another characteristic that distinguishes this southern writer from his peers. Gautreaux thereby inadvertently reminds his readers that race is not the only issue to be explored in the literature set in this region.

Significantly, Deputy Sid here gives the story's "I" a name when "he asked me if I was the Bobby Simoneaux what called." He may be questioning the speaker's identity, but it does not take long for Deputy Sid to recognize him—as in to understand what kind of person he is talking to. In spite of what the two men find—that the man living in the truck "wasn't no old man, but he had these deep wrinkles the old folks call the sorrow grooves" (197) and that "he had been drunk maybe six years in a row" (198)—Bobby insists he wants the truck back. The deputy, the narrator, his daughter, and Fernest Bezue (the thief) drive together to Fernest's mother's house on a road Bobby's own car couldn't travel, according to Sid. While the deputy talks to the man's mother, Bobby's observations reflect much of the story of Fernest Bezue: "While he talked to the woman I looked in the house. All this while my shoes was filling up with water. The first room had nothing but a mattress and a kerosene lamp on the floor and some bowls next to it. The walls was covered with newspaper to keep the wind out. In the second and last room, the floor had fell in. The whole place was swayback because the termites had eat out the joists and side beams. It didn't take no genius to tell that the roof rafters wasn't gonna last another year. A wild animal would take to a hole in the ground [or perhaps an old truck] before he lived in a place like that" (199). And still Bobby insists that Fernest should be put in jail for stealing his truck.

From his narrative perspective, telling about telling the story to the priest, Bobby describes the deputy's reaction to his persistence: "Sid looked at me hard with those oxblood eyes he got, trying to figure a road into my head" (199). By noting that tax dollars would be wasted on Fernest, Sid does convince Bobby this time, but when the truck is stolen again, even though his wife has told him he must get rid of it, Bobby calls to report it—directly to Deputy Sid—and Sid tries reason and compassion rather than just money. But when Sid notes that the narrator has another truck, Bobby's reaction is to suggest that the "pomade Sid been smearing on his head all these years done soaked in his brain." Bobby is also unmoved, apparently, by Sid pointing out, "You got a nice brick house, a wife, three kids, and two cars . . . you might quit at that." Later, when Sid finds the truck and confirms that it has once again been stolen by the same man, in response to Bobby's outrage Sid "looked at me like I was the thief" (200). Sid then remarks, "Simoneaux, you play with those old people like they your own *grandpère* and *grandmère*. You don't know what they done wrong in they time," which gets Bobby to worrying, "Maybe I was nice to the old people because I was paid for that. Nobody was paying me to be nice to a drunk Bezue." Here Bobby starts to get at the root of his "confession," and here again, then, in the retelling, he interrupts himself to bring the priest back into the story, "frowning a little now, like his behind's hurting in that hard-bottom chair, but he didn't say anything, still didn't look" (201). So Bobby continues his "confession."

Bobby reports that he went out to find Fernest and his truck (since Bobby had decided not to press charges, Sid can't call in a tow truck). He "wanted to do the right thing," Bobby says, but when he finds Fernest, just before a storm yet still lying in the back of the truck "waiting for lightning," he decides, "that's how people like him live, I guess, waiting to get knocked down and wondering why it happens to them" and also that "he had what was mine and he didn't work for it, and I figured it would do him more harm than good to just give him something for nothing" (201). So Bobby suggests that Fernest buy the truck from him—for two hundred dollars!—which elicits from Fernest surprise similar to Deputy Sid's over how obtuse Bobby is: "If he had two hundred dollars he wouldn't be sitting in the woods with a five-dollar gallon of wine." Bobby resists further conversation "because I didn't want to get in his head," which the reader realizes is the problem. He can't see the world from Fernest's point of view, as apparently Sid can. So Bobby takes his truck, just as the storm breaks, thus leaving Fernest "standing next to his pile of stuff, one finger in that jug by his leg and his head up like he was taking a shower" (202). At least Bobby begins to have trouble sleeping, indicating that he is beginning to see past the notion of personal insult at having his truck stolen and to recognize that the situation is not just (if at all) about *his* hardship.

The next time the narrator finds Fernest in his truck, it is on his property; Bobby had removed the battery, so Fernest had just fallen asleep in it where it was. Bobby tries again to talk to him, "told him to stop that drink and get a job" so that he could buy the truck, but Fernest just laughs at the naïveté of this suggestion. Bobby is so outraged by Fernest's response that he calls the police again, and though it is not Sid who arrives this time, the policeman who comes, whom the narrator describes as "real country, can't hardly talk American" (that is, a Cajun who speaks in a patois), buys Fernest a ham sandwich before dropping him off outside of town (203). And here again the narrator stops his story to note movement from the listening priest. Perhaps telling of a second person's compassionate response to Fernest, in contrast to his own impatience with the man, jars Bobby out of the past and into the present where the events still trouble him.

Bobby picks his story up again, reporting that he continued to have trouble sleeping because of thoughts of Fernest, which puzzled him since he could also think of "lots of people [who] need help . . . people [who] deserve my help," but then while helping people at the nursing home, he comes across Fernest's mother, living there now that her house finally collapsed. She recognizes Bobby and taps him as "the one" to help her son. Following his reaction to that—"I felt cold as a lizard" and telling the woman "I wasn't going to help no black drunk truck thief that couldn't be helped" (204–5)—Bobby stops again to report on the priest: "He made to swat a mosquito on his arm, but he changed his mind and blew it away with his breath. I didn't know if he was still listening good. Who knows if a priest pays a lot of attention. I think you supposed to be talking to God, and the man in the collar is just like a telephone operator. Anyway, I kept on" (205), reporting that he sought Deputy Sid to help him find Fernest.

The two men find Fernest sleeping in a feed trough, and Sid explains that Fernest had once "passed out on the ground and woke up in blazes with a million fire ants all over him." They wake Fernest, who finally asks the narrator "what I wanted" (206), and Bobby finds himself lying, telling Fernest that Sid bought the old truck for him to live in. Bobby explains in this last part of his story that he'd realized that he "wanted to do something without being paid" (205–6), which is also what he tells Sid to explain his lie. As he wraps up for the priest, though, he says he is still unsatisfied with the experience: "I went home and expected to sleep, but I didn't. I thought I did something great, but by two A.M., I knew all I did was give away a trashy truck . . . mostly to make myself feel good, not to help Fernest Bezue." Bobby reports the priest's response—"He told me there's only one thing worse than what I did . . . not doing it"—and his own response to the priest: "I liked to fell out the chair" (207). While Bobby was clearly not sure what to expect in response to his story, he is surprised by this, and still not quite satisfied, hence the retelling about telling.

There is one more section of the story, in which Bobby reports that upon the death of Fernest's mother, he and Deputy Sid went out to find Fernest but had no luck; then, a couple of months later, Sid called to report Fernest's death—and to give the "gift" alluded to in the story's title, telling Bobby, "We couldn't do nothing for him but we did it anyway" (208). This line, similar to the priest's response, sums up what is admirable about so many of Gautreaux's characters, that is, in spite of the odds against being able to help others, they try anyway. Gautreaux calls his stories like this one "intervention stories": "Somebody's in a bad way, and a character takes that step to help, breaks through the mirror, to go to the other side. There's no story unless somebody does something like that. . . . What propels the story is his decision to help" (Bauer, "Interview").

Gautreaux's choice of metaphors in this summary of the plot of such stories, a mirror, reflects his prototypical protagonist's ability to get past looking just at himself or to see himself in another person and, either way, to take action to try to help the other, which distinguishes his heroes significantly from the Faulknerian prototype, who worries so much about himself that he does not get around to helping others. Gautreaux attributes the selflessness of his protagonists to "being raised Catholic where we have been taught to help people who are less fortunate than we are, not just by praying for them but by actually going out and fixing their busted air conditioners and stuff." He also connects this altruism to his "blue-collar raising. My father never made a lot of money and the people that were his friends never made a lot of money, and when their cars broke down the one of them that was best at fixing cars would go over there and fix it, and when my father's air conditioner broke down the guy in the neighborhood that was best at fixing air conditioners would come over and fix it and it was sort of a quid pro quo relationship among blue-collar workers that way and that's true all over. It's another form of this intervention mentality where you help people for no real reason" (Bauer, "Interview"). This altruistic behavior is found again at the end of the next book, when family and friends risk their lives in a search for the crew of a shrimp boat, and the knight in blue-collar prototypical protagonist will reappear throughout the stories of the next collection.

CHAPTER 3

The Next Step in the Dance

> Colette found it easy to move with him. When she turned and looked down, their steps matched; when she put out her hand, it went right into his on the downbeat. They didn't talk that night, but they did dance.

Gautreaux's first novel, *The Next Step in the Dance*, winner of the Southeastern Booksellers Association Novel of the Year Award, is set in 1980s south Louisiana, just before and then following the collapse of the oil industry, a significant period in Louisiana history, which Gautreaux experienced personally and feared would be forgotten:

> I was born and raised in Morgan City, Louisiana, which is an oilfield town. And the entire oil industry in Louisiana crashed and burned during the eighties. I saw the effects firsthand: the out-migration of white-collar people and skilled workers, the idle boats and oil rigs, and so many people out of jobs, houses that were worth two hundred thousand dollars going down to ninety thousand dollars in value overnight, just about. I could see it happening around me, and nobody else was writing stories about the oil bust. I'm sure people who experienced the Dust Bowl in the thirties had the same feeling: is anyone going to write about this? I felt that if I didn't produce literature out of this, maybe nobody else would. There are lots of events in American history that are ignored and unknown because nobody wrote anything about them. And I had the feeling that this

was going to happen. People talk about the oil bust as an economic phenomenon, but *The Next Step in the Dance* shows it as something that affects people in a very painful and personal way. It's one thing to say that twenty thousand jobs were lost; it's another thing to put a reader inside the house of one of those people who lost his job.[1]

At the center of *The Next Step in the Dance* is a young couple, Paul and Colette Thibodeaux, childhood sweethearts who have been married eighteen months at the novel's opening and are finding themselves at cross purposes, Colette wishing to settle down and save some money in order to have nicer things and Paul wanting to extend his partying years with more middle-of-the-week late-night drinking and dancing, often erupting into bar fights. Coming from blue-collar families, both Colette and Paul work to make ends meet, Colette in a bank and Paul as a machinist, but Colette is ambitious for both of them and wishes that Paul had turned his talent for bringing machines "back from the dead" to the medical profession (21). Paul is satisfied with his work, enjoys it even, and his ambition is limited to becoming "a better machinist" or, if pushed by his wife to aim higher, "the best machinist in the world" (12). In this novel, then, Gautreaux examines Louisiana's laissez-faire attitude from another angle, quite different from the critical tone he took in "License to Steal," although it is interesting that the novel's opening does to some extent echo the opening of this perhaps most negative of his short stories, as, not far into the novel, Colette leaves Paul and Louisiana for California.

But Paul is no Curtis Lado (of "License to Steal") and does not seem to be heading toward becoming Curtis when he's older. He may enjoy partying, but he also holds a regular job and is very good at what he does. In contrast to Colette, he is happy where he is, even as he sees that "something about Tiger Island was slightly out of balance, a little too littered, sun-tortured, and mildewed" (16). He accepts the place for what it is: "Oil country. Fish country. You don't wear a suit to those jobs and you don't listen to Beethoven in your truck" (23). When Colette calls his attention to the "mud and snakes and piles of roadside garbage. Little burned-out fishermen," Paul responds, "Now how the hell would you be eating these big crabs if it wasn't for them little burned-out fishermen" (22).

While Gautreaux says that he "very seldom put[s him]self in a story"—and this may be one of the secrets to the great success of his short stories—he does also admit that Paul Thibodeaux "seems to be my alter ego" and adds, "Paul would be the closest to how I feel about certain things."[2] In particular one can find Gautreaux's deep love of his home and all that it encompasses—the place, the people, the Catholic Church, the food and other elements of the culture—reflected in this young man's devotion to his home and family.[3] While Gautreaux resists being termed a southern or Cajun writer, he notes that one trait that identifies southern writers as unique is that "southern storytellers seem to love where they are from, warts included."[4]

The reader's sympathies go back and forth between Colette—hearing about her husband dancing with other women and then catching him at a drive-in with one—and Paul—criticized by his wife for not being ambitious enough—but the scales tilt in Paul's favor as he follows his wife to California even though he has no desire to leave the home that he loves. Paul's behavior has heretofore reflected a resistance to "the next step in the dance," that is, the responsibilities of a married man. As noted, he has continued to go out at night, even when his wife is not up to going with him after a long day's work, and he continues to end up in barroom brawls, still acting like an adolescent boy rather than a husband and potential father. The final straw for Colette is finding Paul with a woman at the drive-in, and though he may be telling the truth when he says they were only there to see the movie, it is still inappropriate, still evidence that he doesn't understand what being married means. He deserves the come-uppance of his wife's departure, and, shocked into awareness that he may have destroyed his marriage, he leaves the home he loves to try to win back the woman he loves.

Paul's behavior in California confirms the potential that Colette recognizes in the man she married. It may not be a good time for her to leave Louisiana (it turns out that her mother is having small strokes and her father is experiencing episodes of dementia), but it *is* time for Paul to grow up. As a husband he could become a father, and as a father he must be a better role model than some philandering (if only in appearance) barroom brawler. In the California chapters of the novel, Paul exhibits other qualities that one would value in a husband and father: patience, as he does not chase his wife when he arrives, allows her the space she seems to need at this time, but is there for her when she calls; ethics, when he finally refuses to lie about an inspection that would drive an immigrant owner of a laundry out of business; and loyalty, to his wife by not fooling around and to his family back home, keeping in touch while he is gone. Colette, in contrast, neglects her family once she is away, finding it too painful to talk to them as she tries to remake herself, especially as she finds her new life less glamorous than she had hoped.

Both being talented young people, Paul and Colette do well in the work they find in California—until each is fired: Paul when he tells the state inspector that his boss made up the report on Mr. Wu's boiler and Colette after she responds to a co-worker's sexual harassment with a clipboard to his head. By this time the glitz has worn off of California for Colette, and when news comes of her mother's death, she goes home to take care of her father.[5] Now it is Colette who will do some necessary growing up. Following a dream based on "*Cosmopolitan* and *Woman's World*" (2), she deserted not just a husband who may have deserved it, but also her parents. Colette now has to live with the guilt of not being there to help her mother, whose strokes suggest the hard work that sent her to an early grave, and Colette's loss and guilt are compounded by the fact that she is pregnant (with Paul's child, the result of a night they spent together in California).

Colette and Paul both find Louisiana in dire straits upon their return, the kind of economy that reflects *why* people ultimately have to grow up. Jobs are scarce and a baby is on the way. Colette has dreams reminiscent of Scarlett O'Hara's after the war: "Poverty invaded her dreams. One night she was stealing food from the back of a truck. On another night she dreamed she was shooting rabbits with her father's .22 pump rifle and then cleaning the animals in her kitchen" (143–44). Memories of fine meals in California restaurants prompt her to accept dates with Bucky Tyler, whom the reader can recognize as untrustworthy from his first appearance to court Colette, especially given that he has a grudge against Paul who bested him in a humiliating bar fight one night early in the novel. Colette takes a job in the office of Bucky's surprisingly successful industrial sanitation business and also recommends Paul when Bucky needs an expert machinist.

Colette may enjoy dating this still prosperous man as an escape from the poverty all around her, but she also still takes her marriage vows seriously, even though by this point she is legally divorced: "She was Catholic and couldn't remarry. This prohibition gave her a cynical joy, an excuse not to get tied down to another man" (143).[6] But Bucky has other ideas, so when Colette tells him, "I can't get married because of Paul. It's against my religion" (162), Bucky plans Paul's death by coercing him into a boiler to do an inspection and then trapping him inside after hours. Here Gautreaux incorporates the plot of an earlier "literary detective novel" he had drafted but never published.[7] The intrigue, in spite of the melodramatic element of attempted murder, fits well into the novel's overall conflict development, as Colette must recognize her own role in the near death of Paul. She had perceived that Bucky saw her as some kind of "a prize" and understood that "he would be such a dreadful husband with all his east Texas backwoods views of women and how they should have big hair, look good, and shut up" (162), but she blames her religion for her resistance to his advances while enjoying the perks of the relationship, not apparently having learned from her California experience that the direct approach would have been better. There too she had responded coyly at first to her co-worker's sexual advances, which he candidly tied to her career advancement in the bank. The last time the villain was hurt, but this time an innocent victim, Paul, is almost killed, and Colette realizes the connection between the danger Paul had been in and her own attraction to glitz and glamour: "This suffering was her fault, she realized. . . . She was at a crossroads where she could marry a man who stood a chance of becoming powerful and rich one day, or she could do something else—she didn't know what, just that it could involve hard times, bad food, and cheap clothes" (176). This climactic event in the novel, powerfully narrated and, with Gautreaux's own knowledge of machinery, vividly rendered to keep the reader turning the pages as Paul struggles to get out of the boiler in which Bucky has trapped him after everyone has left for the day, occurs in the center of the novel. It is, not surprisingly, a key turning point in Colette and Paul's relationship, though it does not conclude with their reconciliation.

The reader enjoys Colette's revenge on Bucky: she finds incriminating evidence in his files of how he has violated federal pollution laws for big payoffs from industries for whom he provides waste removal services. As an added bonus, he does not realize it is Colette who turned him in until he calls her from jail to ask her to go into his office and destroy the evidence he knows can be found there. Colette is ultimately a very strong woman, the likes of whom Bucky could not appreciate. As the second half of the novel unfolds, she directs that inner strength toward feeding her family while simultaneously helping Paul to recuperate from his ordeal, which has left him somewhat crippled and thus no longer the dancer he once was, both literally and figuratively. At this "crossroads" in her life, Colette has chosen, if not Paul directly yet, at least the way of life she grew up living, even if it does mean "hard times," and she is now wincing at the waste of her California money on the Mercedes she drove while there. She is "embarrassed . . . to realize how much she liked money, thought about money, yearned after shiny things in general" (183). For strength against the temptation these material things are to her, she reaches back to "her mother's advice [on] how she should always remember God, become educated, choose a good man and a good job that would allow her to live comfortably," now realizing that "comfortably" did not necessarily relate to wealth (182).

Paul also may have reached to his faith for comfort when trapped in the boiler, but, physically weakened by the ordeal, he suffers a kind of posttraumatic depression upon his release from the hospital and finding himself with a new baby to help support—yet jobless and unable to find work as a machinist with the loss of dexterity resulting from his injuries. Compounding his sense of impotence after his injuries, he can't fix either Colette's car or his father's, and he seems to blame himself, alluding to how his past behavior led to his current situation when he remarks to Colette about having to walk over to help her with her car: "'Might as well walk. . . . Can't dance anymore. . . . Can't get in any trouble'" (184). But here again Colette recognizes her own role in his suffering and determines to help him: "She had caused Paul to lose more than she'd realized, and she decided it was her job to help him get something back" (185). So the next time she solicits his services, it is to help her with something he *can* do—borrow his grandfather's boat and take her out to hunt nutria rats for their pelts. And with this Gautreaux begins the novel's next adventure, which once again builds to a climactic brush with death, this time with Colette as the near-victim.

As this episode of the novel unfolds, Paul and Colette get back in touch with their Cajun roots. Paul recognizes that *Grand-père* Abadie "never had any more than he has right now. He's poor and doesn't know it. We used to have some money. That's what hurts" (193). With this realization, Paul is on his way to the kind of enlightenment Colette has been experiencing since the birth of their son. Paul can also take a lesson from Abadie's boat, which hasn't been used in years: "As long as he had a boat, he was still a fisherman. Without it, he would just be an old man" (194). And when the young couple seeks out the old man, Abadie and the priest visiting him give them a history lesson about their respective ancestries, reminding them of blood relations who survived harder times than what they are currently enduring.[8]

The nutria hunt is successful, Colette being a good shot, but when she gets too greedy and they stay out longer than they should, dark falls before they can get home and Paul runs over a cypress knee, pitching Colette into the water. She is knocked out, and though weakened by his recent injuries, Paul goes into the dark water to find her before she drowns. Again Gautreaux's gripping narration, this time with vivid details of the swamp setting, compel the reader through the pages to Paul's rescue and resuscitation of his wife. When he tells Colette what happened, she asks him how long he swam before finding her: "As long as I had to," he responds, and she then asks, "How could you?" (210), alluding to his own weakened state and thus suggesting to him that he is not less of a man, as he had suspected. But Paul ends up back in the hospital, the exertion being too much for his still convalescing body, in spite of which Colette ignores his insistence that he's too tired, "tired past the bone" (219), and continues her endeavors to push him back to the "hard work . . . you love" (216). While he is still laid up, she shares her latest scheme of buying a bigger boat and becoming fishermen.

Poverty and guilt are taking their toll on Colette, who pushes herself "to fish much harder and smarter than anyone else. Asking questions, studying tides, moving locations daily, she brought in as much as the middle-aged men who'd fished all their lives" (225), even as she worries about her son, Matthew, after several close calls, including one time that she falls onto a snake and, to keep it from biting her, grabs hold and does not let go until another fisherman hears her yelling and brings a knife to kill it. In the boat one day, she observes her surroundings from a perspective similar to Paul's early appreciation of his home, warts and all: "She imagined that all towns had a hell of a lot of ugliness in them and that people still chose to stay there, listen to the wind in the trees at night, sit on the porch in the dark and wonder at the empty street. Maybe Paul had been right about California and it was only a place for a vacation, a place that kept you away from blood kin if you moved out to stay" (232).

While Colette has honed her sharpshooting skills to hunt nutria, dickered with a salesman until he sells her a boat motor she can afford (using what Paul has told her about motors to stop the salesman from condescending to her as a woman), and wrestled with a snake, Paul is still suffering from literal as well as emotional impotence. And since he has confessed his condition to Colette, it is likely that her next money-making scheme is as much about reminding him of his earlier, more virile days as it is about money, for with "her darkest, sweetest smile" directed at Paul "for the first time in years" (237), she wheedles him into going with her to the seediest of bars so that she can participate in a five-hundred-dollar-prize shooting contest, where, as Paul suspected would happen, a fight breaks out and he must not only hold his own but also get her out of there unhurt—which he does.

With this episode, too, Gautreaux continues his characterization of the culture, which is as much a part of this novel as the relationship between Paul and Colette. Talking about this novel with interviewer Maria Hebert-Leiter, Gautreaux remarked, "Some people read the novel and ask, 'Well, what's the point?'" His answer is to call the book "a tribute to a culture."[9] Certainly such scenes as the afternoon at this bar, as well as the previous hunting and fishing episodes, capture "the [Louisiana] culture as it was in the 1980s [with] elements of the 70s, and 60s, and 50s"—indeed, Gautreaux notes, "particularly all the fist-fighting scenes." Gautreaux explains his motivation: "I found that if I didn't nobody else would. There aren't many people down there writing 'literary' fiction about blue-collar Cajun culture" (Hebert-Leiter, 71–72). True, but in 1979 folklorist Dave Peyton, noting the continued absence of the Cajun perspective in literature up to that time, predicted a novel like *The Next Step in the Dance* when he remarked that "the best Cajun literature will come from telling the stories of the death of the culture itself."[10]

Hebert-Leiter notes a tension she finds in Gautreaux's fiction regarding "taking pride in Cajun culture." Responding to this interviewer's question as to why it is the women in his fiction (like Colette) who experience this tension most profoundly, Gautreaux points out that the "women [he] was raised around were just like Colette" and that "life was very hard for women in the 1950s, in that Louisiana was a poor state. . . . The women had to be very tough, and they also had to assert their dominance in the family." Reminding the reader of the novel's beginning, he continues, "The Cajun mother was very influential and strong. . . . If she was a push over, she had a miserable life. So she had to run the finances . . . of the family and keep her husband in line. . . . Sometimes she had to be pretty rough with her husband to get him to behave. This attitude . . . was passed on to the daughters, because I remember even on the playground the girls were pretty darn mean. They would throw rocks at you. If some girl was especially interested in you, she would throw a big rock at you" (72). Colette is certainly rough with Paul, from leaving him when he tries to prolong adolescence after their marriage to pushing his convalescence along so that he is unable to succumb to the temptation to give up on himself. When forced to face the fact herself that her husband has finally "'grown up a lot,'" as her aunt points out to her, and is not just staying home nights because the bars are closed, Colette must also answer her aunt's question about her own maturation ("How about you?" [255]). If she too is a mature adult, then it is time to reconcile with her husband. Regardless of their divorce, they are still married in the eyes of their church, and she seeks Paul out, "giving off vibrations like a friendly Judgment Day" (258), and "began to explain things—what she wanted in the next five years or so for herself and Matthew" (259). When he expresses doubts—"I'm not a hundred percent. Sometimes I don't feel like a man. . . . I'm not making a joke when I say I might not be man enough for you anymore" (260)—she just takes care of that issue with a kiss, seeming to bring the novel to a fairy tale ending in which the princess awakens the prince with the magical kiss.

But the novel is not quite done. The whole community must first be brought into one last dramatic event when Colette challenges Paul to win her back by "figur[ing] something out where we can put our money together, maybe a business or a service, something that could grow, something that would support us so we could buy decent clothes, a car that runs, a meal out once a week" (260). Together the two decide to buy a shrimp boat, and forming a crew of other unemployed friends and relatives, Paul takes up his wife's challenge to the point of risking the crew members' lives when they once again stay out too long to make another pass for shrimp one day with a storm pending. When they do not return,

> Colette knew she was going to do something important, though she had no idea what, but she felt it coming, the way she knew the next step was coming up in a dance, the music propelling her toward the inevitable motion. She felt her will swell up and move the flesh along her back, because

everything she had sensed and thought about Paul in her life came funneling down to this moment, this dot in time, and at once she knew what she was going to do. In that instant, she knew she loved him. It was the knowing what to do that told her.

She ran into the house, saw the kitchen telephone, and took the next step in the dance. (299)

Colette calls the father of one of the crew members to help her search, and they are joined first by two of Paul's bar brawling friends, the Larousse twins, and then by other relatives. They find some of the crew, but not Paul, and the reader wonders if Colette's realization that she loves him has come too late. In spite of this probability, Colette understands that even "if they had found no one, the search would have been worth it, because such a group would form for her only one place on earth" (326), this community that she once deserted. As Gautreaux has noted, "Sometimes you don't know how you fit into your community until you leave it."[11] Colette's various efforts to feed her family have earned her the respect of her community, and they will continue the search for Paul as long as she asks them to, even as they are already beginning to eulogize their missing loved ones. But she too finally accepts Paul's apparent death, thinking "of how hard Paul must have tried to stay alive in all this water, and why" (326) and thus recognizing that this time again his presumed fate is largely her fault. Then *Grand-père* Abadie arrives, having gone out in his old boat and found his grandson and the other missing shrimper after what was a grueling night on the water for the old man. As Paul had told Colette after she nearly drowned, you do what you have to for those you love, and doing so, as Paul has learned, is what makes you a man, the secret, it seems, to Abadie's longevity.

Tim Gautreaux has nicely summarized this novel's themes in an interview with Christopher Scanlan: "It's about the moral decision you make when you abandon your roots, your class, when you think you're better than your raising. . . . It's about bailing out of a marriage that could be fixed, and about what it means to be in a relationship for the long haul. . . . When young people get married, they have no idea what marriage is about."[12] Paul and Colette know now, and the reader accepts the happily-ever-after tone of the scene's closing laughter, Colette's loudest of all, as Paul worriedly tells Colette he "'lost the boat,' . . . his voice full of fear and shame" (338), and then of the short ending chapter of Paul waking up to a new day some time later, listening to his world around him, the description broadening from his perspective to include his wife in bed beside him and a reference to their son and "a new girl-child" (339) and to *Grand-père* Abadie sitting next to him in church later that morning; then Colette at her desk back at a bank job, looking at photographs of her parents, "loves she had escaped in spite of her best self," listening to the train "rattling back from California": "For a long time she stared with her quick dark eyes at where the train had come from, at the blue-black rails that trailed off to the west. Then she looked down at the iron roofs of Tiger Island. Some were storm-worn and bent, some eroded and rusty, porous as a ruined soul, and some were scraped clean and gleaming with new silver paint" (340).

Gautreaux has said of the influence of Walker Percy upon his writing, that Percy "was not very opinionated as to what we should write about, but he was very adamant in letting us know that we're all on some kind of a quest. . . . The characters are always looking for something . . . for what makes them happy"

(Hebert-Leiter, 67). Colette and Paul went all the way to California and came back to find happiness exactly where their parents and grandparents did—at home, with family. The novel's conflict resolution may be considered somewhat romantic, but it is not sentimental. Rather, the happy ending reflects Gautreaux's nostalgia for the values of the Louisiana he grew up in, which could help to preserve the Cajun culture threatened by the exodus of so many Louisiana natives after the 1980s oil bust. Gautreaux does not idealize his home region, but he does respect it, and he regrets the inevitable loss of what distinguishes it. Writing this novel in the second half of the 1990s, Gautreaux would already have witnessed malls and fast-food chains taking the place of downtown shopping and local restaurants, even in small-town south Louisiana, but as he once remarked about the focus of his fiction on his native region, "I just try to go back to what I remember, and when I feel I'm losing touch, I go off to Fred's Lounge in Mamou on Saturday morning and listen to the band and watch 'em dance."[13]

CHAPTER 4

Welding with Children

> I'm not exactly sure how I do it myself, but it's a con-
> scious mixing of comedy and tragedy, of irony and
> straight non-ironic storytelling. A lot of it's like tap
> dancing or jitterbugging or singing: either you got it
> or you ain't.

Commenting on "the notion of hopelessness or despair that I see in a lot of contemporary fiction," Gautreaux asks, "Where are the short stories about the small successes that people have dealing with their problems?" (Bauer, "Interview"). Such is one of the literary holes his stories fill as his characters, never too old to change, continue to try to make a difference in the lives of the people around them. And magazine editors and writers selecting the "best" stories continue to appreciate his contribution to the genre. Stories that would appear in his second collection, *Welding with Children*,[1] were first published in top literary magazines. "Easy Pickings," for example, first appeared in *GQ* and was then selected for *New Prize Stories 2000: The O. Henry Awards*. "Welding with Children," "The Piano Tuner," and "Good for the Soul" were all selected for *The Best American Short Stories* after their appearance in the *Atlantic*, *Harper's*, and *Story*, respectively. *New Stories from the South* chose "Sorry Blood" in 1998 and "Dancing with the One-Armed Gal" in 2000, and "Rodeo Parole," first published in *Georgia Review*, was picked for Gautreaux's appearance in the southern literature anthology called *Voices of the American South*.

"Welding with Children"

> I guess a lot of what's wrong with my girls is my fault, but
> I don't know what I could have done different. (7)

Same Place, Same Things ends with the only first-person story in
the collection. Gautreaux's second collection of stories, *Welding
with Children*, begins in the first person. Like his debut volume,
this collection opens with the title story, and Bruton, the story's
narrator, is another manifestation of the most common Gautreaux protagonist, a character who accepts responsibility and
acts to improve the life of another, whom he has no *obligation*
to help. As in "The Courtship of Merlin LeBlanc" and "Little
Frogs in a Ditch," Bruton finds himself responsible for his grandchildren. In particular, as in "Little Frogs," he takes it upon himself to try to influence their moral character, though in this story
the children are so young that perhaps Bruton will be more successful than Mr. Fontenot is.

Though Bruton's daughters, unlike Merlin LeBlanc's children,
are still alive, they all, like Merlin's daughter, have illegitimate
children, and Bruton recognizes as the story progresses that these
four unwed mothers' behavior (which resulted in these children)
can be traced, at least in part, to his own detached fathering.
Bruton's awakening begins when he finds himself responsible for
the four grandchildren his daughters have ("typical[ly]," he says)
dropped off for their mother to watch on a day when his wife
had plans to go to the casino. Introducing Bruton's bewilder-
ment over his daughters' values, along with a reflection of their
economic circumstances, he also reports that one of the young
women brought a broken iron rail from her bed for him to weld
back together: "Now, what the hell you can do in a bed that'll
cause the end of a iron rail to break off is beyond me, but she

can't afford another one on her burger-flipping salary, she said, so I got to fix it with four little kids hanging on my coveralls" (1). It is an eye-opening day for him, a day when he realizes, as a *grand*father, how trying it can be to have four children underfoot, and the reader should keep in mind that he is a *father* of four children himself. Traditional though it may have been during the youth of his own children for the fathers not to be involved in the daily care of children, Bruton suddenly recognizes the resulting burden upon his wife, a working mother: "LaNelle always worked so much, she just had time to cook, clean, transport, and fuss." Consequently, he now recalls, "the girls grew up watching cable and videos every night, and that's where they got their view of the world, and that's why four dirty blondes with weak chins from St. Helena Parish thought they lived in a Hollywood soap opera" (7). As Gautreaux explains for this story's appearance in *The Best American Short Stories 1998*, Bruton is "typical of grandparents all over who are raising their grandchildren, maybe because they didn't raise their children right to begin with. Most of them try to do better the second time around."[2]

Bruton's introspection is prompted not only by the evidence around him (the broken bed and the four children) of his unmarried daughters' sexual activity and his grandchildren's unselfconscious use of profane language but also by the judgment of the local chorus, a group of town elders who sit outside a convenience store where he takes the children to buy a treat. Just as he turns the engine of the car off, he overhears one of them remark, "Here comes Bruton and his bastardmobile" (4), which sets him to wondering about his daughters' morals. There had been no time for "religion" when his children were growing up, and he now realizes they had not "pick[ed] it up from their mamma, like I did from mine" (7). So he asks the children whether their mothers talk to them about God, and hearing that they only hear God as part of "cussing," he finds a Bible storybook to read to them, noting, "It was time somebody taught them something about something" (8). But their world is so defined by what they have seen on television that the serpent talking to Eve reminds them of cartoon animals, and the armed angel banning Adam and Eve from Eden of *Conan the Barbarian*. "The Bible was turning into one big adventure film" (10), Bruton realizes. While one child remarks in wonder that he thought that animals only talked on television, another counters the story of Abraham and Isaac bitterly, saying, "Daddies don't kill their sons when they don't like them. . . . They just pack up and leave" (11).

Bruton is so disgusted by his grandchildren's reaction to the Bible that he "formed a little fantasy about gathering all these kids into my Caprice and heading out northwest to start over, away from their mammas, TV, mildew, their casino-mad grandmother, and Louisiana in general. I could get a job, raise them right, send them to college so they could own sawmills and run car dealerships" (like the children of the man who had denigrated him in town). But then he looks down at his shoes, "paint-spattered and twenty years old," which remind him he "ha[s]n't held a steady job in a long time," all of which illuminates for him the harsh truth that "whatever bad was gonna happen [to these children] was partly my fault." Looking around him, he then wonders anxiously if his wife has ever entertained a similar escape fantasy, "leaving her scruffy, sunburned, failed-welder husband home and moving away with these kids, maybe taking a course in clerical skills and getting a job in Utah, raising them right, sending them off to college." Indeed it is likely that his daughters have also fantasized escape from this place.

But, he finally realizes, "we couldn't drive away from ourselves. We couldn't escape in the bastardmobile" (12). The best he can do at this point is cut the circuit to the television and read the children a story about a heroic dog.

To the reader's surprise, the next day Bruton seeks the advice of the old man who had made the cutting remark the day before—significantly seeking Fordlyson out under the locally named "Tree of Knowledge" in the middle of town. He confronts the old man, saying, "I need help with those kids, not your meanness" (14). Fordlyson cuts off his idea of talking to his daughters about their children. It's "too late for their mammas [like Mr. Fontenot's grandson in "Little Frogs in a Ditch"]. . . . They'll have to decide to straighten out on their own or not at all" (14). Instead he offers advice for what to do about the grandchildren: take them to church—not Bruton's fundamentalist church but a mainstream church with a good children's program.

It is interesting to note in Fordlyson's advice about churches that he mocks Catholics, "some of [whom] don't put more than a dollar a week in the [collection] plate" (15). Like O'Connor, Gautreaux is Catholic, but his characters are not all Catholics, and the Catholic Church is not spared his satirical pokes. Still, as L. Lamar Nisly notes, the humor in this story (and Gautreaux's others), is not harshly sardonic. In his *Christianity and Literature* article on Gautreaux and O'Connor, Nisly uses this story to show the difference between the two writers' attitudes toward their audiences, noting Gautreaux's "gentler tone": "His cordial relationship with his audience leads him to . . . a conversational approach with his readers. Unlike O'Connor, who feels compelled to confront her hostile audience, Gautreaux sees his audience as made up of fellow travelers. Gautreaux's imagined audience, it seems, consists of people who recognize the difficulties in life but, because of their Christian faith, do not see the world as finally brutal and hopeless."[3] Fordlyson does not believe that Bruton will follow through on trying to improve his grandchildren's moral consciousness: "You'll go home and weld together a log truck, and tomorrow you'll go fishing, and you'll never do nothing for them kids, and they'll all wind up serving time in Angola or on their backs in New Orleans" (15). Bruton insists he will follow the old man's advice, so Fordlyson continues, telling him to "clean up your yard," advice that perplexes Bruton, but Fordlyson insists, "It's got everything to do with everything. . . . If you don't know [why], I can't tell you" (16).

Bruton doesn't know why, but Fordlyson's daughter does arrive to pick up her father in a Lincoln, so Bruton goes to see the Methodist preacher and then home to start on his yard: "The next morning, a wrecker and a gondola came down my road, and before noon, Amos loaded up four derelict cars, six engines, four washing machines, ten broken lawn mowers, and two and one-quarter tons of scrap iron" (16). After Bruton cuts grass and paints the house, his bemused wife asks what's going on and advises, "Careful you don't paint yourself in a corner," worried, apparently, that he will start something he can't finish (17). If she understands what he is doing, she knows how much work is ahead for him. But then one of their daughters arrives to drop off her baby and her nephew, and Bruton agrees readily to take care of the boys. Handing over her own child, she tells her father that the baby said his first word, "Da-da," and leaves in tears over the sad irony. Bruton, to his credit, notes her distress and calls for her to wait, but perhaps Fordlyson was right about it being too late for her: "In a flash, she was gone in a cloud of gravel dust, racing toward the most cigarette smoke, music, and beer she could find in one place" (18).

The older grandson also left in Bruton's charge notes the changed surroundings and asks his grandfather, "What happened . . . ?" (18). Bruton merely responds that he is going to put up a tire swing. The reader recalls that on that fateful first day in their grandfather's care the children had tried swinging on an engine hanging from a chain until they got distracted and let its nine hundred pounds swing into them, knocking this boy down. This incident, following Bruton's attempt to weld the broken bed with the children underfoot, during which one of the children got hold of the welding wand and zapped him, had shown Bruton that his yard was no playground for children. And looking around at his property that day, he'd wondered how he had let it get so bad. While his brief time in college had not been too successful, he did "make decent money as a now-and-then welder" (2). As the "Bug Man" had noticed about the "Slug" family in the previous story collection, there was no excuse for his surroundings being the mess they were. The reader, along with Bruton, begins to understand Fordlyson's advice about cleaning up the yard.

The reader now also begins to understand the purpose of Bruton's college reminiscences earlier in the story. As a young man Bruton had apparently been ambitious enough to go to college but was embittered by his experience. He recalls feeling out of place on the LSU campus in his "blue jeans that were blue" and around "people that don't have hearts no bigger than bird shot," referring to the fraternity boys who called him "Uncle Jed" and the professors who were condescending to him (3). The old men's attitude toward him is not unlike that of the people he'd met in Baton Rouge, but this time he will learn what he can from Fordlyson, for his grandchildren's sake. Furthermore Bruton might not have passed ambition and religion on to his daughters, but he has passed his intelligence (which got him into college) to his grandson Freddie, who, upon hearing of the tire swing, astutely suggests putting a drain hole in it so it doesn't collect water—testimony to the child's ingenuity. Like his grandfather, the baby is apparently a good judge of character: he turns to his grandfather and repeats his new word, "Da-da" (19). Nisly writes of this ending, "The baby's gurgled words identifying [Bruton] as a father suggest that [Bruton] is taking on a role that he failed earlier with his own children, embracing the morally correct position that he needed to re-learn from his community" (Nisly, "Wingless Chickens," 80). The boy may look at Bruton with "*somebody's* blue eyes" (19; emphasis added)—his father is unknown to Bruton—but the reader believes that Bruton will earn this appellation from his grandchildren in the years to come.

"Misuse of Light"

> Now and then, he'd find something artful or otherwise interesting, and he'd put it in a scrapbook he kept for the purpose. He'd try to figure out what was in the minds of the people in the photographs, but he never could. (23)

In "Misuse of Light" Mel DeSoto is far removed from the issues troubling the young woman who wanders into the camera shop where he works; he is merely a camera repairman and would-be photographer with no relation to the melancholy teenager who brings in a camera to sell, one that had belonged to her deceased grandfather. Mel later learns that the girl has been dealing with depression, aggravated by the loss of this grandfather, whom she adored, but before her mother shares that information, he has inadvertently tainted the girl's memory of the man. Thus does he find himself responsible for her to some extent, and as is typical of Gautreaux protagonists, he does what he can to alleviate her distress.

Like many of the old cameras Mel purchases, this one still holds a roll of film, which Mel offers to the girl, but when she refuses it, he pockets it to develop later, as he often does. "Mel enjoyed the bad photography of amateurs" (23), we are told, just after learning that "as a young man, he had tried his hand at art photography and took courses at Tulane, but his work was not promising, and his professor would write on his projects, sometimes on the photographs themselves, 'Misuse of light'" (22). So apparently he takes some comfort in seeing other unpromising photography, although Mr. Weinstein, the store owner, points out to him that he is "confusing art with reality," that snapshots are "not art" so trying to "interpret" them is just "being . . . nosy" (27).

Not just nosy, Mel is judgmental in his interpretations. For example, from one roll of film he had developed a 1950s-era "color shot of a vacation to the Grand Canyon [with] three weeping little girls in razory focus lined up against the pipe barrier at the edge of a cliff, the canyon itself a Mercurochrome smudge in the background. . . . He showed the photo of the little girls to his wife. She told him that she saw merely tired children at the end of a long ride in a car without air-conditioning. His daughter thought the little girls were spoiled and had just been denied an ice-cream cone" (23–24). It is interesting to note here that Mel's response, like his daughter's, is critical: "Mel suspected an apoplectic father unaware of the irony of driving two thousand miles to record the misery of his offspring against a gorgeous but ignored background. He thought the man was either missing the point of photography or was a very bad person, uncaring about his children's misery and mocking them with a record of it." Mel recognizes that "the photo had meaning, but it was closed. The figures in the paper would not talk" (24). Nevertheless he still makes an evaluation, and it is both condescending and judgmental, neither attitude reflecting the objectivity necessary to interpret rather than impose meaning upon art.

But intent on continuing his endeavors to understand what he sees in the photographs of strangers, perhaps to discover the secret that would help with his own "art," Mel *mis*interprets the story behind the pictures in this particular old camera and in doing so almost destroys a young woman's memory of her grandfather. Noticing that the photographs left in this camera were "carefully composed" and thus considering them "found art," he goes in search of the story behind them, since this is "the first time [he has] a live person connected with a roll of film of this quality" (25–26). Perhaps this time he can find the secret to the art. The girl knows very little about the woman in the pictures beyond her identity. The woman is her grandmother, who died when the girl's mother was very young and who was so much grieved by the husband she left behind that no one talked about her. But with the landmarks in the photograph, Mr. Weinstein helps to place the photographs in time and place, so Mel is able to seek out other sources of information and to discover that the photographs were taken on a riverboat on the very day that it sank. Then, reading the news stories of the accident, he finds out that the woman in the photographs (the girl's grandmother) drowned but that the man who took the pictures (the grandfather) is the man of the headline "MAN SAVES CAMERA, LOSES WIFE" (30).

As noted, Mel misinterprets the "truth" behind this photograph by taking this headline and news story at face value, forgetting the not uncommon occurrence of a news story that does not reflect the reality of events. He comes away from reading this story with a lesson on "the meanings of images: how art can interpret beauty or terror, but ordinary photographs could show only beautiful or terrible *fact*." He puts the newspaper stories together with the photography, "plann[ing] one day to . . . reconcile the two. But not soon," for he is currently distressed by the horrible truth that he believes he has learned about this sad girl's beloved grandfather. If Mel is so troubled by the news, one is not surprised how disturbing it is to the girl, who returns to get the photographs after all, her mother having expressed an interest in seeing them. When Mel carelessly puts the whole folder on the counter for her, the girl is horrified to read that her grandfather "abandoned [her] grandmother for a camera" (31).

The girl's mother is outraged by Mel's carelessness and comes to the store to find out what kind of person is so unmindful of the consequences of his insensitivity. Her response to his attempted explanation is to question his belief that there is a secret that must be deciphered in order to appreciate art: "Think of the Mona Lisa, Mr. DeSoto. If we knew her smile was because she had just been unfaithful to her husband, would that knowledge make the painting greater art?" She also, like Mr. Weinstein, notes Mel's failure to distinguish between art and reality and the consequences when the artistic sensibility forgets that the object d'art is a person: "I can tell you're a certain kind of idiot, and you know nothing about my father. My daughter worshiped him. He was the family anchor, so to speak. I don't know what happened the day my mother died, but now my daughter, who is prone to depression anyway, is distraught, really distraught about what you dredged up. You've done a very bad thing" (33). In contrast to Mel, this woman is not inclined toward a negative interpretation; nor does she immediately accept without question an interpretation that is based on the second that is captured in film but goes against her experience of the *reality* she has witnessed.

Mel is distressed by this call to face responsibility, but again, like Gautreaux's protagonists who recognize their role in another's pain, he endeavors to make things right by investigating the full story behind these photographs. The first thing he discovers, from the accident victim's brother, is that it was the girl's grandmother who was the photographer, not the grandfather (apparently she had at least set up the photographs that she was in). But this source of information is still angry at his brother-in-law for not saving his sister, so Mel can only get that much of the story without bias; therefore he keeps digging—realizing perhaps from the bias of the grieving brother that each storyteller has an angle—and from that realization, that the reporter's angle would have been to sell newspapers. Mel asks a more disinterested source, a deaf man who comes into the store, to read the woman's lips in the last picture on the roll, and this man tells Mel that the syllable her lips seem to be forming is "ga" and agrees that yes, it could instead be "'ca' as in *camera*" (35), which Mel puts together with the knowledge that the boat went down in less than a minute after the collision with a navy ship to mean that it was *she* who was telling her husband to save the *ca*-mera. Mel then invites the girl to meet him at the scene of the accident and on the waterfront shows her the pictures again, noting the expression on the woman's face in the photographs: "She was glowing. She was crazy about him." He explains that according to the brother, the girl's grandmother "was an artist [who] worked as a part-time secretary for ninety cents an hour and saved enough for a Rolleiflex, the best camera in the store in those days. She must have waited years for it," which would have explained her concern about it when they felt the crash (37), but more important, "Your grandfather was what you thought he was. You can see it in *her* face." And finally he advises when he gives her the photographs, "Just look at everything in them—objects, shadows, even the blurry parts. . . . You'll see" (38), he says, having realized himself the importance of getting the full story before making assumptions.

"Good for the Soul"

> He suddenly thought of an old homily that told how people were like twin-engine planes, one engine the logical spirit, the other the sensual body, and that when they were not running in concert, the craft ran off course to disaster. (52–53)

In "Good for the Soul," Gautreaux puts the priest hearing a confession at the center of the story rather than employing him as a sounding board, as he does in "Deputy Sid's Gift." As Gautreaux explores his academic profession a bit in "Navigators of Thought" (and will again in a couple of stories in this collection with academics at their center), he takes a critical but empathetic look at his religion in this story. He seems to be questioning, at least as a tangential concern of this story, the consequences of the celibate life the Catholic Church requires of its priests, as their solitary home life sometimes results in substance abuse. Related to this candid look at Catholics' spiritual leaders, Gautreaux reminds his readers that while, as Father Ledet points out in the story, priests are the mediators of God as they hear confessions, they are also very much human beings, who may have as much trouble living up to their parishioners' high expectations as any other human being would (and the alcoholics among them would have as much trouble as any other alcoholic does giving up alcohol).

This story begins with Father Ledet enjoying a drink after a pleasant and satisfying meal prepared for him by "sweet women of the parish [who] had fed him pork roast, potato salad, and sweet peas, filling his plate and making over him as if he were an old spayed tomcat who kept the cellar free of rats." This last image suggests a source of dissatisfaction in the priest over his lifestyle, which may be related to his drinking, for, juxtaposed against the neutered cat image is his physical description, which includes the detail of his "huge spotted hands that could make a highball glass disappear" (39). After they feed him, the women go home, and Father Ledet is left alone for the evening. A drink of brandy after a fine meal leads to several drinks to pass the time, but as a priest he is always on call, and sure enough, he is summoned to the hospital to give last rites. Father Ledet considers telephoning his housekeeper to drive him, but averse to having "the old Baptist woman" sniffing his breath, he "felt his mossy human side take over" and drives himself (40–41). With this allusion to the priest's pride, Gautreaux reminds his reader again of the human nature of the priest, whose role in society is supposed to be beyond reproach but who, underneath the collar, is a man after all.

Set up against the representative of God's law in this story is the keeper of man's law, Patrolman Vic Garafola, who is on the scene when "his own parish priest" runs into Mrs. Mamie Barrilleaux, who suffers a broken arm in the accident (41). Vic smells the liquor on Father Ledet's breath, so while he agrees to take him on to the hospital to perform the last rites, he also waits around to take him on to the police station from there. While he waits, Vic "wondered what good it would do to charge the priest with drunken driving" (46), which is the same question that the dying man asks Father Ledet about hell. After confessing sins back to the time of the Cuban missile crisis—apparently the last time he felt his life threatened and thus wondered about divine retribution—Clyde Arceneaux asks the priest if there really is a hell and whether "it's for punishment." Father Ledet says that, yes, that is what he believes hell is for. "But what good would the punishment do?" asks the old man. Father Ledet responds, "I don't think hell is about rehabilitation. It's about what someone might deserve," but then he adds the consolation that "you shouldn't worry about that, Clyde, because you're getting the forgiveness you need" (44), which prompts Clyde to confess his last sin, having once stolen a car from his brother-in-law. Clyde sees having to state the confession out loud as "some of that punishment we were talkin' about earlier. It's what I deserve" (45), which is what Father Ledet will need to do as well—face public acknowledgment of his crime.

Clyde's crime is relatively benign. He stole the car because it had no muffler and his brother-in-law, who lived in his neighborhood, would run it early every morning and wake the whole neighborhood. It was a nuisance, so Clyde hid it in a storage unit. Father Ledet's crime is, of course, not so humorous, as evidenced by Mrs. Barrilleaux's broken arm, the painful setting of which Patrolman Vic takes Father Ledet to witness when the priest emerges from the old man's room. So the policeman writes up a ticket charging the priest with driving under the influence, and Father Ledet has his license suspended and loses his insurance, consequences of the secular world. While still in the hands of earthly law himself, Clyde starts considering how to make amends for his crime, and he decides he wants to return the car. His wife, however, does not want him to die with the reputation of being a thief, so they call on Father Ledet to return the car for them so that the thief might remain anonymous.

The farcical nature of this request leads the priest to wonder: "His years in the confessional had taught him that people did not run their lives by reason much of the time, but by some little inferior notion of the spirit, some pride, some desire that defied the simple beauty of doing the sensible thing" (49). Of course, once again this insight could be turned on himself, for being too proud to admit that his driver's license has been suspended leaves Mr. and Mrs. Arceneaux wondering why he refuses to help them. They send Mrs. Barrilleaux to remind the priest, with her arm in a cast, of his own fallibility, and he agrees to return the car in an effort to make up to her for the injury he has caused.

The tension of waiting until past midnight to return the car causes the priest's legs to ache, and he goes in search of aspirin, but approaching the cabinets where the aspirin is kept, he is drawn to the brandy that will soothe his nerves: "The mind and the spirit pulled his hand to the right [toward the cabinet with aspirin], while the earthly body drew it to the left [where the bottle of brandy was kept]" (52). Several drinks later he sets out for the car. Once again Patrolman Vic is on the scene as Father Ledet drives the old car, with its expired plates, from the storage unit to the owner's neighborhood, and again not knowing who the driver is who has turned off his lights upon entering the neighborhood, Vic turns on the police car's flashing lights and siren, resulting in a car chase—comical except for the fact that the inebriated priest might have hurt someone else if not for the hour (at which there were few people on the road). When the chase is finally over, in front of the car owner's house, Father Ledet tries to get the policeman to turn off his flashing lights and lower his voice, but it is too late, the neighborhood is awakened to the public "confession."

Father Ledet pleads with Vic to "have some mercy" and notes again that "this won't do anyone any good," but once again the theme of getting what one deserves is repeated. "Them that deserves it get mercy" (56), Vic tells him. And in fact Father Ledet is ultimately treated mercifully, if not by the police or the church or his neighbors, all of whom condemn him, then by his God. After his two-month suspension from his church, during which he has to attend AA meetings at which he must endure one confession after another, upon returning to the pulpit, where he faces the cold, unforgiving faces of his parishioners, he looks out and sees Clyde Arceneaux inside the church, "something that was better than forgiveness, better that what he deserved, something that gave sudden light to his dull voice and turned bored heads up to the freshened preaching" (58–59). It seems that Clyde at least, whose confession included "missing Mass 'damn near seven hundred fifty times'" (44), found in Father Ledet's experience a reason to come inside. While the others seem to have expected the priest to be immune to temptations of the flesh, Clyde apparently finds a flawed human being at the front of the church worth coming inside to hear; Father Ledet, he recognizes, is someone who can understand his own weaknesses and thus might be someone worth listening to after all. The fallible priest, in turn, feels the relief that comes after confession, and the reader believes he is absolved.

"Easy Pickings"

> Anyone who would live out here would be simple, he thought, real stupid and easy pickings. (62)

"Easy Pickings" is a fun story employing elements of southwestern humor. Deputy Sid returns to the scene of the crime in this story, but this time the intended victim is refusing to be victimized. Eighty-five-year-old Mrs. Landreneaux cannot be easily intimidated: "You want to hurt a old lady what had seven children, one come out arm-first?" (63), she asks the man who tells her he is called "Big Blade." Apparently she recognizes the "small, petty, and dull" Marvin hiding behind the hyperbolic moniker (62). Her reaction to his crab, scorpion, and lobster tattoos, while giving the reader a chuckle, is certainly not what Marvin expects: "Baby, who wrote all over you?" (62), she asks him, then mocks him further with "You with the crawfish drew on you throat, you trying to scare me wit' a knife? Like I ain't use to death?" (63), thus inciting the blow that sends her dentures flying across the room. But still she shows no fear, having over the course of her long life killed with her own hands (chickens), as well as lost loved ones and nearly died herself; she gets up to feed him rather than fetch the money he has demanded.

While Doris Landreneaux is making company out of a would-be thief, her neighbor on this isolated road, Sadie Lalonde, is enjoying a game of cards (bourrée again, the game played in "Died and Gone to Vegas") with "three widows and one never-married man" (65). The card players notice the strange car parked in Mrs. Landreneaux's driveway, speculate on whose it might be (not the right make of car to be her son's), then consider whether it might belong to a Jehovah's Witness. The reader relaxes into the comic tone and waits to see who will end up with the money, both the money on the table and the money Marvin is hoping to find in Mrs. Landreneaux's house. Gautreaux transitions casually between these two groups of characters until they all meet in the middle, outside, for the showdown.

Back at Mrs. Landreneaux's house the phone rings, and Big Blade tells Mrs. Landreneaux to "act normal [or] I'll cut you open," but Mrs. Landreneaux casually answers Mrs. Lalonde's inquiry about the visitor, explaining that her guest is not a

Jehovah's Witness but "some boy with a sword trying to rob me like the government." Hanging up, she again blows off Marvin's threats, reassuring him that "Sadie and that gang playing bourée. You couldn't blow 'em out that house with dynamite" (67), and offers dinner to her "terrorist" as she walks away to check the chicken stew she remembers is on the stove. Mrs. Lalonde hangs up on her end, not sure "what to think" but not too concerned. "She'll talk the intrudin' parts off their body, that's for true," Mrs. Breaux remarks (68). And the reader, privy to both scenes, realizes she is right, that the card players apparently know Mrs. Landreneaux pretty well.

Since there seems to be no danger, the reader is not concerned when "the old women [playing cards] turned toward Mr. Alvin, a tall, jiggly old man with pale, fine-textured skin who was built like an eggplant. His pleated gray trousers hung on him like a skirt on a fat convent-school girl" (68). The description amuses, as does the idea of this man being the knight they send to the rescue, and events continue to progress toward a tall tale–like ending as Mr. Alvin sneaks next door to peak into Mrs. Landreneaux's window and find out what's going on inside. When Mr. Alvin rushes back, scared by the knife he saw and the threat he heard to "put [Mrs. Landreneaux] in that stew pot" (69), they call Deputy Sid to come to the rescue (wearing the cowboy hat he wore in "Deputy Sid's Gift"), but at the same time Mrs. Lalonde gets out a shotgun and Mrs. Breaux finds the right caliber shells to load it with. The police officers don't take the call too seriously—more amused by "Mr. Alvin . . . looking in a *woman's* window" (72) than concerned about the intruder story—but Deputy Sid is sent over to find out what is going on.

All this time Mrs. Landreneaux is feeding Big Blade / Marvin, who is so "stunned with food, drowsy, dim-witted with food" (72) that he doesn't notice Deputy Sid walk up until he is standing in the door. Still Mrs. Landreneaux remains calm, inviting the deputy in for coffee, even as Marvin grabs her and threatens to cut her throat (Marvin, in contrast to his intended victim, is startled by the striking of a clock). Deputy Sid puts down his gun as instructed by Marvin but then casually picks up Marvin's knife and drops it out of reach. He speaks quietly to Marvin, explaining his situation—swamp to the south, rice fields to the north, his car out of gas because he left it out idling all the time he has been inside making his threats and eating.

So Marvin takes Mrs. Landreneaux, Deputy Sid's gun, and the police car, and the story proceeds to a comical car chase. Seeing police cars in front of him, Marvin believes he can just put the gun to Mrs. Landreneaux's head and they will let him pass, but, still levelheaded, Mrs. Landreneaux fakes a heart attack, and Marvin suddenly worries that burglary and kidnapping are about to turn into murder and get him the electric chair, so he heads back to her house. Upon his return the card players shoot out one of his tires, and when he tries to shoot back at one of them, he discovers that Deputy Sid's gun is not loaded. Apparently Deputy Sid gave Mrs. Landreneaux credit for being able to take care of herself but had acted so as to protect Marvin from himself.

Once Deputy Sid reassures everyone that more police are on their way, Mrs. Breaux puts down the gun and expresses her excitement over getting back to their game, inviting Mrs. Landreneaux and the deputy to join them and then turning to Marvin with an invitation to come play cards with them "if you ever get out of jail" (77). She recognizes "easy pickings" when she sees it.

"The Piano Tuner"

> The piano tuner was the kind of person who hated for any-
> thing to go to waste and thought the saddest thing in the
> world was a fine instrument that nobody ever touched, so
> it made him uneasy that someone who could play like this
> lived alone and depressed in an antique nightmare of a
> house ten miles from the nearest ear that knew what the hell
> her fingers were doing. (83–84)

The title character of "The Piano Tuner" is a knight in blue collar reminiscent of the "Bug Man" in *Same Place Same Things*. I
have argued elsewhere that this story can be read as a revision of
Faulkner's "A Rose for Emily" in which Gautreaux replaces
Faulkner's anonymous first-person narrator with a man willing
not just to stick his nose into the business of a lonely heiress by
reporting it but also to stick his neck out to help her—before it
is too late to *do* anything for her.[4] Answering a service call, a
piano tuner named Claude finds Michelle Placervent in need of
more than a piano tuning; the woman is seriously depressed. Her
situation directly echoes that of Faulkner's Emily Grierson. She
is "the end of the line for the Placervents, Creole planters who
always had just enough money and influence to make themselves
disliked in a poor community." After her mother's death,
Michelle had to take care of her father, who had started drinking, and after his death, "it was just her, the black housekeeper
[who has since died], the home place [which is in disrepair], and
a thousand acres the bank managed for her" (80). Michelle has
a music degree but "had never done anything, never worked
except at maintaining her helpless mother and snarling old man"
(81–82). And, also echoing details in Faulkner's story, "she
had been engaged twice, but old man Placervent was so nasty to

the young men, he just ran them off" (90–91). The stasis of Michelle's life is reflected in her desire for a new piano, thwarted by the condition of her house, so rotten that the steps wouldn't hold to move the old one out. Claude suggests that she move, but she "can't afford to" and besides, the house is the only family she has (84).

Gautreaux noted during one interview that he had first written this story with a female piano tuner, but then changed the character to a male, creating "this lovely thing—a relationship between a man and a depressed woman, where there could be some kind of sexual attraction, but they have enough self-discipline to realize what an awful idea it would be." Thus, he continues, "the tuner offers her help not based on that psychosexual need that most people write about."[5] It is also interesting to know that Gautreaux himself once worked as a piano tuner. From that experience he learned that service people are more likely to "see us as we really are. They are not 'company,' and we don't greet them at the door with the polite façade we use for friends and relatives. We tend to be franker with them." Writing for *The Best American Short Stories 1999* about his own experience as an inspiration for this story, he explains that "people would talk to me while I was in their homes [tuning their pianos], and I could tell whether they were happy or sad. If I'd ask them a personal question, they would generally unload their histories on me. After all, whom could I tell? What did I care? Who was I, anyway?"[6]

The piano tuner in this story is moved by Michelle's talent when she plays for him and troubled by the waste, not just of her talent but of her life. Typical of the Gautreaux serviceman protagonist, Claude does not just brood about Michelle's situation; he eventually gets involved. During his first service call, he asks outright, "What problems you having, Michelle?" (82); when she calls him about more stuck piano keys, frantic that he come right away, he again asks her directly "if she had any relatives or friends in town" (87), makes her tea, then, after adjusting her piano, continues to pry into her troubles, coercing her to see a doctor. Once she is on medication, Claude finds her a job playing the piano in a motel bar, even advises her about what to play and how to dress, and promises to be there on her first night. Whereas Michelle's ultimate triumph occurs upon her own initiative, certainly it is Claude's prompting that sparks her later intentional or fortuitous break out of her confinement.

When Michelle first comes to see Claude about helping her to find a piano-playing gig, while he is pleased by her progress, there is something troubling about her countenance: "Her eyes showed so much happiness, they scared him" (89). He is concerned that this "happiness" is too much connected to her medication. Then, during her first night's performance, the manager remarks to Claude, "She's smiling a lot. Is she on something?" (93). More portentous, at one point that night, just after Claude left, he heard her break into Hungarian Rhapsody no. 2, and when he goes back in to find out why she was suddenly playing music so inappropriate for a lounge setting, she tells him, "I couldn't help it. I just got this surge of anger and had to let it out. . . . I've been sitting here thinking that I would have to play piano five nights a week for twenty-three years to pay for the renovation of my house." And then she asks, significantly, "What am I doing here? . . . I'm a Placervent" (93). Significant, too, when she pulls herself together, she returns to the piano and sings, "Crazy . . . crazy for feeling so lonely" (94).

But Michelle continues to play in this motel lounge, as well as at the Sheraton and the country club, though she also continues

to end many nights somewhat hysterical, "laughing out loud between the verses as though she were telling jokes in her head,"
and when he hears of this, Claude "wonder[s] if she would ever
get on an even keel" (94). Upon finishing the story, the reader
wonders if she might have been devising her escape from her
imprisoning house and was laughing in anticipation of the sce-
nario described in the closing pages.

The next time Claude is called to her house it is to tune a new
piano; she'd done just enough renovation so that her house
would support a delivery. But the music store didn't want her old
piano and wouldn't haul it away for her. Perhaps it was only
then that circumstances inadvertently led to the story's end
(rather than it all having been premeditated), although the cheap
ugliness of the new piano, noted by Claude, suggests that it
could have been part of her scheme.[7] By the time of Claude's
arrival, Michelle is preparing to pull the old piano out the back
door by hitching it to the tractor her father forced her to learn
to drive when she was a child.

The earlier tractor reference in the story, which seemed
insignificant at the time, suddenly becomes very significant,
reminding the reader of how a good short story writer does not
include unnecessary information. After his first service call to
Michelle's house, when Claude told his wife about how depressed he'd found her and shared his opinion that she should go
to work, to his surprise his wife responds, "Well, she knows how
to drive a tractor" and explains that she "heard that [Michelle's]
father forced her to learn when she was just a kid. . . . Maybe
he was mad she wasn't born a boy." Then, foreshadowing the
story's end and suggesting how we are to interpret the events
that ultimately transpire—as intentional demolition rather than
accidental destruction—Evette answers Claude's hyperbolic "I

wouldn't have thought she could operate a doorbell" with "It might surprise you what some people can do" (86).

What Michelle ultimately does is singlehandedly tear down her prison. After hitching the piano to a "locomotive"-sized tractor, "the only [tractor] in the barn that would start" (or so she says), Michelle tells Claude, "*I've planned this through*. You just stay on the ground and watch" (96; emphasis added). What follows *seems* like an accident. The piano turns broadside en route, and when Michelle gets down off the tractor (presumably so that she and Claude can turn the piano sideways again so that it will fit through the door), her raincoat catches on the clutch, engaging it. Claude pulls Michelle out of the way and then the two watch as the tractor continues to drag the piano out of the house, from its broadside position, so that it brings with it the door frame and consequently the entire back wall. The back rooms collapse, then the roof, all while the tractor continues to drag the massive piano; and while Claude wonders if he should try to stop it but then stays to support the collapsing Michelle, a fire erupts from where the gas stove would be, underneath the rubble.

Michelle seems genuinely shocked—it's hard to believe she could have imagined such a scene even if she did plan any part of this debacle—but when she is questioned by the fire chief (who perhaps feels bad since by the time the firemen arrived it was too late for them to do anything but wet down the camellias and live oaks on the property), she responds, "The only good thing the house had was insurance" (98), again leading the reader to wonder about her intentions (recall that the new piano inside, which is presumably destroyed, was "cheap" and "ugly" [95]). Then later that evening she says to Claude and Evette, "Look at me. I'm homeless," and the narrator follows her words with "But she was not frowning" (99). She even laughs when they hear a story on the news about a runaway tractor that tried to pull a piano up the steps of a Catholic church and declares of the piano, "It escaped" (100). Whatever her intentions were, the result was the same: like the piano, Michelle has escaped her prison.

Michelle may remain a little "off" even after her escape (she still does some odd talking at times during her sets), but thanks to Claude's constructive intrusion into her life, she is no longer isolated, and she is not completely mad, as Faulkner's Emily seems to have been. The last we see of Michelle, she is still playing the piano in the motel lounge and has attracted a following of regulars. Without the financial burden of the house, she is gainfully employed as a lounge singer, and she is no longer living isolated ten miles from her nearest neighbor. In contrast to Faulkner's narrator, who helps us to understand Emily Grierson but only after she is dead and it is too late to do anything that would improve her life, Claude's intrusion into Michelle Placervent's life has helped the victim, not just eased his own conscience. And in this story Claude is not responsible in any way for Michelle's situation, again unlike Faulkner's narrator, who is part of the "we" who have watched Emily over the years and speculated about her various disappointments but have *done* nothing to console her.

"The Pine Oil Writers' Conference"

He read nine pages, thinking how much better than this he could have done. He kept reading, with each page his mood sinking down, down. He read on even after the counter girl started to bang her little bell repeatedly, calling out his name to please come on and claim what was his. (120)

Just as the tone of "License to Steal" reflects an impatience with Louisiana's failure to value education, in "The Pine Oil Writers' Conference" Gautreaux reveals a bit of disdain for some elements of the writer's world. This story mocks the writers' conference at which more attention is paid to socializing than to writing. Ultimately, though, the story is more about writing than it is a criticism of writers. Gautreaux shows in the end that talent is not enough (and sometimes not even necessary). The writer must also have self-discipline and motivation to take advantage of talent and, sometimes, to make up for the lack thereof. This story also further explores the wasted talent theme of "The Piano Tuner," but in this case the main character is at the start motivated to take advantage of his writing talent, which he has recently become aware of, but then sinks back into the depression he might have, like Michelle Placervent, used his art to rise above.

The setting for most of this story is a writers' conference. The protagonist, a Presbyterian minister named Brad, who has discovered an inclination to write and a modest talent for it, seems to be the one participant of this conference there to find "that magic, holy thing all writing hopefuls sought: The Answer" (104). The other participants "were buying the fantasy of being writers, but as long as the booze and the sad, emotionally famished companions held out, the only things they would ever write would be checks to lower-echelon writers' festivals all over America" (110). And the writers leading the discussions and workshops are not much better; they seem more interested in fighting with each other over theories about writing than in teaching the paying customers to write. So while Brad's roommate focuses on scoring with other conference participants, Brad asks out the one teacher who has published numerous novels—not seeking a conference fling with a writer but to have a chance "to talk about writing" (111).

This writer/writing teacher, Faye Cooker, does distinguish between two types of writers' conferences, "one where people wanted to learn to improve their writing, and one where people wanted to get drunk with published authors, overeat, and get laid" (111), and she does help Brad turn his experience into the former kind even as everyone around him seems to be enjoying the latter. Behind her advice to Brad one may hear Tim Gautreaux answering the kind of questions writers get at the more productive kind of writers' conferences. In one of their early conversations, Faye asks Brad what his novel will "say," explaining, "I like to think of the novel as a voice" (108). She also advises him to "start with your family, something they did either last year or last century. Something your old man told you, or your grandfather" (108–9). And to his saying he thought he'd try detective fiction, she asks, "Are you a detective? . . . Anybody in your family a detective? A best friend? An acquaintance? A ninth cousin?" (109). One hears here the old standard but no less true "write what you know" that the author/professor must have told his students countless times. Later the story's teacher adds further advice would-be writers often hear from published writers: "Keep writing until you think you know where you could go with the tale, then stop and plan. Then rewrite, rewrite, throw the first thirty pages away, and rewrite again, sentence by sentence" (112). The reader wonders if the author himself has repeated this advice so often he decided to find a way to record it for future reference and decided that publishing it as part of a story and showing by example was more practical than an essay on writing would be.[8]

Beyond the writer's advice on writing, this story does exemplify through other elements of short fiction—that is, character development, conflict, setting—the advice it provides. Illustrating what makes him a master of the genre, Gautreaux reveals in the limited space of the short story details of his character's past that flesh him out and directs us to recognize the true nature of the conflict, which is not, after all, that of a frustrated writer only lately discovering his talent. We learn that "a year ago [Brad] was having stomach problems, his wife was thinking of divorcing him, and he had just been transferred to a smaller church." Note how this last detail so succinctly implies how he was failing in his work. Employing his typically unromantic imagery, Gautreaux adds, "He got up early one morning to empty his bladder, and he felt a similar liquid weight in his soul." The feeling inspires him to sit down and write—not a sermon but a short story "about a man quitting his job and buying a motorcycle to escape the South." Certainly the story reflects a fantasy Brad might have, but he is still writing from his own experience—of the desire to just quit, if not the actual quitting. Brad then sends the story out, and when it is accepted by a minor literary magazine, he finds in that acceptance the impetus to write more—and he is rewarded with more publications as well as with the return of his wife's interest in him. Hence the motivation, too, to seek some instruction in his new avocation: "Brad imagined that locked up inside him somewhere was a novel that would dazzle the world, or at least create a few sparks in his hometown" (104).

Gautreaux thereby subtly implies that Brad's desire to write reflects his desire to be noticed and appreciated by his wife and by his community. Interestingly Brad is not (and neither is Gautreaux) blaming them for not noticing him. Rather he suspects that he is somehow to blame: "He worried that he might have a talent that he was wasting, and that he could be called into account for this in the next life, that God might be someone like his burly uncle Ralph, who had given him a circular saw twenty years ago and who never failed to ask, 'Hey, boy, you makin' something with that saw I give you? You keeping oil on it?'" (104). The reader learns of Brad's tendency to store it away rather than use what comes his way when Faye Cooker responds, "Thank God for that," to his comment about his grandfather not being "very interesting" (implying that he is not an interesting subject for literature). She is telling him another "answer" about writing, which Brad "absorbed . . . and shrugged . . . off at the same time." Gautreaux explains, "He was a man who appreciated truth by storing it away, like coin collectors who keep their treasures in a bank box and haven't seen them for decades" (109).

Even before the conference Brad was realizing he needed to let his treasures out for air and appreciation, and at the conference he learns that he does have a talent. Upon reading the material Brad writes during the conference, Faye Cooker tells him something she has "never told anyone" before him: "I think you should quit whatever it is you do for a year and finish this novel," and she offers to help him find an agent when he is done. Then, when he asks her to tell him what is "wrong" with his story (with the same negativity as his guilt for the wasted talent), she responds instead, "Let me tell you what you did right, and how to keep doing it for years to come" (119). In this story, his own version of the parable of the talents, Gautreaux explores a moral issue behind his own writing: "I actually believe it would be evil for me to not do what I can do well. Whatever you can do well is a gift, and if you don't exercise it, then you're doing something wrong. That's one of the main reasons I write."[9] With Brad, then, Gautreaux explores what might happen should someone waste such a talent, and one might say that this story has one of the least hopeful endings of any of Gautreaux's short fiction.

While the writers' conference ends positively for Brad, he does not go home and write his novel. He did go home "on fire to create," feeling that "he had found The Answer," but then he seems to have fallen back—and pretty quickly—into the same doldrums that had motivated his first story, only this time he is not inspired: "He could write well and so what?" (119). The reader may expect to hear, then, that he channeled the positive feedback he had gotten into his sermons, but rather, we hear that Brad's congregation is no more moved by his sermons than they apparently were before. His wife, who had been impressed by his dream and by his apparent potential for success, is disappointed by his failure and divorces him after all.

In a bookstore ten years later, Brad sees a novel by his conference roommate, Butchie, who had been more interested in partying than writing and who had received a harsh response to the material he turned in for critique. On the back of the novel is a picture of Butchie with the same woman he had an affair with at the conference, a woman whom Brad suspects has written much of Butchie's novel for him—or perhaps this is just sour grapes—in any case the writing is still bad. While the final revelation of Butchie's publishing success may be Gautreaux's poke at some of what finds its way into print, the reader is more concerned about Brad's failure, typical as it is of so many dreams. Brad was right to be concerned about wasting a talent, but he does not have to wait to be punished in some afterlife for not making good use of God's gifts. His punishment is reflected in the unchanging tenor of his life. Except for the brief high he experienced while he was writing and the even greater elation of hearing from Faye Cooker that his writing was good, he is still weighed down in his soul.

"Resistance"

> "So what are you going to call this project?"
>
> "Resistance." She said the word as though it had another meaning.
>
> "And we gotta figure out how to demonstrate it, right?" He closed his eyes and thought back to those late-night projects of his children. (126)

"Resistance" may remind the reader both of stories such as "The Bug Man" and "The Piano Tuner" and of stories such as "The Courtship of Merlin LeBlanc" and "Welding with Children," the former pair because the blue-collar hero steps in to try to help a damsel in distress (this time a preteenage girl) although he bears no responsibility at all for her troubles, the latter pair because he is an older man (almost eighty, older than the other grandfathers who have served as unlikely heroes), retired, widowed, but still willing to *take* responsibility for doing something to stop, or at least lessen, the suffering of a someone in this case almost three generations younger.

The story begins with the establishment of a *new* New South setting. Alvin Boudreaux lives in "a tiny subdivision built in the 1950s, when everybody had children, a single-lane driveway, a rotating TV antenna, and a picnic table out back." Still a porch sitter in spite of air conditioning, Alvin has noticed that there are now two (usually compact) cars per house, "one for each spouse to drive to work" (121). Dual incomes are one sign of the changing times; another he notices later is that people cannot hear their neighbors' domestic squabbles over the hum of air conditioners, which is dangerous if the squabbling escalates to violence.

The reader may consider the idea that one reason Alvin has "outlived his neighbors" is his willingness to go along with the changes he witnesses around him, even as he is "in that time of life when the past began coming around again, as if to reclaim him" (121). While his observations may reflect a preference for earlier, more neighborly times, Alvin does not dwell on the past and in fact feels he should trade in his large Buick for "something that would fit in" better (124).[10] He may be approaching eighty, but he is living in the present, neither looking to the past nor anticipating his death. Alvin also seems unburdened by regret. When he decides to get involved with the unhappy child next door, he does not seem to be making up for past mistakes with his own children, though the reader comes to realize (along with Alvin) that he is repaying a debt—paying forward a gift from his own father so that the neighbor child might experience that kind of expression of love.

Alvin's watchful nature comes in handy when he notices the girl next door, Carmine, trying to get her father to help her with something and then overhears the mother trying to persuade her husband to do so as well, since what the child wants involves "electricity . . . something a man'll have to do" (123). Unlike Bruton of "Welding with Children," Alvin seems to have been engaged enough in his children's lives to know about science project time, and seeing the child's acceptance of her father's rejection and hearing the mother telling her husband "weak[ly]," "You're her parent, too" (123), he uses his experience to start up a conversation with the girl that leads casually up to him helping her: "'It's springtime,' he said. 'My kids used to have to make their science projects this time of year'" (125). Then, when Carmine shows up that afternoon, he casually fixes her a Coke float before they begin, and the reader feels that this is likely not the first after school snack he has produced or at least he knows that an after school snack is in order.

Readers may notice Carmine's failure to thank Mr. Boudreaux for the treat, but she does get up and put her glass in the sink, and as the story progresses, one theme that develops is the idea that children should live in a family in which such niceties as a coke float can be expected by children from the adults in their lives. Noting Carmine's failure to express gratitude, L. Lamar Nisly suggests that "Gautreaux's presentation of this unresponsive girl gives the story a level of believability and offers a helpful corrective to the too-common sentimentality found in stories: Not every child who is helped by a caring adult is cute, articulate, and immediately rewarding. In fact Gautreaux's portrayal of Carmine seems to be his way of suggesting that children—indeed, everyone—intrinsically are worthy of caring attention, not only the beautiful ones who make their way into Hallmark movies" (Nisly, "Sacramental," 142).

Talking with Carmine as they work, Alvin remembers that when he was a child, an assignment snuck up on him, and, noticing his anxiety, his father asked him about it. The assignment was to build something from the novel *Great Expectations*, and after telling his nearly illiterate father about the novel, Alvin woke up the next day to find that his father had built for him the prison ship in the novel. Alvin concludes his story, "The old man was like that. . . . He never asked me if I liked the boat, and I never said anything to him about it, even when I brought home a good grade for the project" (132). Again the reader notices that no thank yous were offered, which may seem unusual in a story that seems somewhat nostalgic for simpler, politer times when lending a hand to help a neighbor's child did not, as happens in this story, lead the father to call the police to find out if

Alvin is a child molester. But Gautreaux's point seems to be—at least what Alvin seems to realize as he helps this child—that the real sadness is not the often self-centeredness of children who expect generosity and thoughtfulness from their parents but rather a child's meek acceptance of her parents' failure to be generous and thoughtful. It is not until he witnesses Carmine's "patience" (122) when her father rejects her appeal for help that almost-eighty Alvin comes to understand what a blessing his own father was. The adult Alvin is briefly troubled by the memory of his failure to express his appreciation to his father for his help, but then feels "that by helping with the science project, he had completed something important and that he and the girl had learned something" (133).

The girl's enigmatic reaction to the help she receives from her neighbor may keep any moral lesson she has learned somewhat mysterious or, as Nisly suggests, may leave the reader wondering, in spite of Alvin's suggestion here that she too "had learned something," if she has recognized his help as "a sign of God's love" and how she will respond to it (Nisly, "Sacramental," 146). But Alvin's involvement means to him a "resistance" to his inclination toward giving in to what Nisly describes as "the mindset of the neighbors around him, people who seem to find little to value or invest in deeply," including children: "Mr. Boudreaux's self-giving actions underline the intrinsic value of each child" (Nisly, "Sacramental," 144). After completing the project Saturday night, Alvin goes to Mass Sunday morning with a light heart, feeling like "a conduit of God's love," but the good feeling that comes from having "offer[ed] up . . . his achy back and his tired legs for this forgotten girl next door" (Nisly, "Sacramental," 145) is interrupted when he comes home to find Carmine's father drunk and furious that his neighbor's help had made him look bad. The science project is destroyed, and the drunk man knocks Alvin down before his wife pulls him away. That night, sore and angry, Alvin determines not to give up on the lesson, the payback to his own father's memory. He spends all night re-creating the project, having to take apart the television and a hi-fi for bulbs and knobs, as well as borrow switches from his electric saw and barber's clippers. He must also suffer physically to complete the work. Alvin, usually in bed by eight, spent a second late night, this one an all-nighter (the previous one occasioned by Carmine explaining they had to finish before Sunday, when her father expected her and her mother to hang around quietly while he drank in case he needed something). Alvin even cuts up a new hose in order to siphon gas from his car for the blowtorch they had used for soldering, thus sacrificing not just old things he no longer needs but something he can still use.

As his father had done for him, Alvin stays up all night, rebuilding the project itself, as well as typing up the report from Carmine's discarded drafts (on one of his own daughter's old typewriters) and reproducing the posters she'd made. The next morning he follows her school bus with the completed project. When Carmine sees what Alvin has done, she checks it over for accuracy and then takes it from him with only an expression of concern that she will be late if she does not go in. Again she expresses no gratitude, but this too replicates his reaction to his father's help. The difference may be that this child has not been taught to say thank you, but also she may not have been taught to expect anything she might say thank you for. Alvin's father seems to have helped his son out of concern for Alvin's anxiety over an oversight that could get him into trouble; Carmine's father simply refused to help her, and in a few places in the story the reader discerns that his treatment of her is at least somewhat related to a disappointment over having a daughter rather than a son. When his wife pleads with him to help Carmine, he responds, "Why can't she do something like a girl would do? Something *you* could help her with" (123), and when Alvin tells Carmine he has two daughters, she responds, "What would anybody need with two girls" (128).

In this light Carmine's knowledge of such electrical terms as "resistance," which she has chosen for her project, and of tools such as a soldering iron takes on a poignant significance: the reader wonders if her interests might arise from the desire to make up to her father for not being a son. In any case the reader understands that the man's disappointment might have been lessened if he had opened his eyes and realized his daughter had interests he could relate to. The reader witnesses, for example, the child's awe over Alvin's workbench. Caught up in his narrow view of gender roles, Carmine's father is missing out on how he might enjoy his daughter if he put down his bottle and paid attention to who she is. As he works with Carmine, Alvin relives "for a minute [being] a younger man, looking down on the head of one of his own daughters." And in direct contrast with Carmine's father's rage over looking bad in front of his family, Alvin feels "expert as he guided Carmine's short fingers and held the circuit board for her to thread the red wire through to the switch terminals. He felt back at work, almost as though he were getting things done at the mill" (131).

Alvin has certainly accomplished something in this weekend of working with and then *for* young Carmine. He has revealed to this neglected child that selfless generosity does exist in the world and that she, a daughter, can be the beneficiary of such. As Nisly suggests, the story shows "a trail of goodness, that helpful patterns as well as hurtful ones can be passed from one generation to the next" (Nisly, "Sacramental," 145). In celebration of his renewed commitment to being involved in the present, Alvin returns to the idea of trading in his car but stops off at a store to buy plastic flowers that remind him of his mother's jonquils, and he takes them to his father's grave, "this place where no one would say the things that could have been said, and that was all right with him" (139). Untroubled by Carmine's failure to say thank you, Alvin recognizes from his own experience, as Nisly puts it, "that her lack of verbalized thanks does not indicate ingratitude so much as an inability to put into words what she is thinking" (Nisly, "Sacramental," 145). The focus in the story is ultimately more on Carmine's role in affecting Alvin's life, much as the sullen young woman serves to lead the much less likeable Mrs. Turpin in Flannery O'Connor's "Revelation" to her vision of the last entering first. We do not know how Carmine has interpreted Mr. Boudreaux's help, but we do know that helping her has helped Alvin: "No longer is he merely fretting over his neighborhood going to ruin; he has found a new ability to live deeply in this world and in so doing to encounter another reality as well" (Nisly, "Sacramental," 148). Alvin has seen evidence of God's grace.

"Sorry Blood"

> Then he again scanned the house and yard, which would never be worth looking at from the road, would never change for the better because the very earth under it all was totally worthless, a boot-sucking, iron-fouled claypan good only for ruining the play clothes of children. He thought of the black soil of his farm, his wife in the field . . . he thought how far away he was from anyone who knew him. (154)

In "Sorry Blood," Gautreaux explores domestic violence again, but this time two untraditional forms of abuse: a wife physically abusive toward her husband and his abuse in turn of a parent figure (though not his actual parent). The story begins in a Wal-Mart parking lot, where an old man first forgets where he parked and then, "one by one, things began to fall away from the morning, and then the day before, and the life before" (141). This line, which so perfectly captures what it must be like for the person slipping into dementia, shows Tim Gautreaux at his best. A short while later Gautreaux inserts another detail that captures the fear of the Alzheimer's victim: "The old man wanted to feel his head for fever, but he was afraid he would touch a stranger" (143). As the old man wanders around the parking lot, a man in one of the parked cars calls out to him, asks him what's wrong, and then identifies him as the younger man's father, which the old man accepts "like a fact" (142).

The reader, however, is instantly suspicious: "The man in the Ford smiled only with his mouth" (142) when he encourages the old man into his car, then immediately asks for "my wallet, the one you took in the store with you" (143). The trusting old man hands it over and they drive away. As the younger man, Andy, drives toward "home," Gautreaux's expertise with detail turns toward capturing the depressing landscape: "After a few miles, he turned off the main highway onto an unpaved road. . . . Then the gravel became patchy and thin, the road blotched with a naked, carroty earth like the hide of a sick dog. Bony cattle heaved their heads between strands of barbed wire, scavenging for roadside weeds. The Ford bumped past mildewed trailers sinking into rain-eaten plots. Farther on, the land was too soggy for trailers, too poor even for the lane's desperate cattle. After two miles of this, they pulled up to a redbrick house squatting in a swampy two-acre lot. Limbs were down everywhere, and cat-briers and poison oak covered the rusty fence that sagged between the yard and cutover woods running in every direction." Upon arriving Andy "pull[s]" the old man from the car, feeling his arm "for muscle" (143) and promptly puts "his father" to work digging a ditch to drain water from the yard, eventually (after several margaritas) explaining that his wife "told me she'd beat me again and then divorce my ass if I didn't fix this yard up." The reader figures out more of what is going on when Andy mentions that, expecting his wife back soon, he "went to the discount parking lot to hire one of those bums that work for food" (145).

While the old man does not yet suspect that Andy has lied to him about his identity, he does see that the younger man is "desperate," so he cooperates as best he can. He doesn't remember any details about his life, but he can tell that he "ha[s] used a shovel before—his body told him that." In contrast, even as Andy complains about the "lazy bastards" who "won't work" (145), he lies around drinking margaritas the first day and starts drinking beer early the next morning. In between, the old man becomes "dimly aware that where he was, he had not been before," and again Gautreaux's imagery vividly captures the dementia experience: "His memory was like a long novel left open and ruffled by a breeze to a different chapter further along" (146). He accepts his current situation before lying down to sleep—"My name is Ted. I am where I am" (147)—but whatever his name is or isn't, he is also who he is, so when he wakes up to find "his son" watching pornography (significantly, involving a woman being whipped), he reacts as the reader guesses he would if he found a genuine son of his enjoying such filth: First he responds verbally with "Only white trash would watch that," and when the message doesn't phase Andy, he "hit him from behind [with] a roundhouse open-palm swat on the ear that knocked him out of the chair" and repeated, "White trash . . . No kid of mine is going to be like that" (147), demanding that Andy turn off the television. Andy cowers under the rage. A typical Gautreaux character, the old man then takes some responsibility for Andy's behavior: "Maybe you've got from me some sorry blood," he tells his son. Then he encourages him to "let the good blood come out, and it'll tell you what to do. . . . You can't let your sorry blood run you" (148). In her review of this collection, Erin McGraw notes that the title of this story, which comes from this passage, "recalls [Flannery] O'Connor," and the story's "plot links moral outrage to wild, angry humor, every bit the equal of O'Connor's in the depravity of its characters. And like O'Connor's, Gautreaux's vision doesn't flinch."[11]

The next morning Andy sends the old man out to work again, explaining that he is too sick to work himself. While "Ted" continues his ditch digging, Andy reads the newspaper, which includes "a brief account of an Etienne LeBlanc, a retired farmer from St. Mary Parish who had been staying with his son in Pine Oil when he disappeared." The story explains that the missing man's "spells of forgetfulness . . . had started the previous year on the day [his] wife had died while they were shopping at the [same] discount center" where Andy had found "Ted" (150). It isn't too long before Etienne LeBlanc also discovers who he is, significantly via his memory of his deceased wife. Going inside for water, the old man studies the kitchen, knowing it "was some woman's kitchen" but feeling that it was "like no place a woman should have" (151). Later, worrying over a splinter he got from running his hand over the bare kitchen shelves, his memory comes back: "Paper, the old man thought. Shelf paper. His wife would have never put anything in a cabinet without first putting down fresh paper over the wood, and then something came back like images on an out-of-focus movie screen when the audience claps and whistles and roars and the projectionist wakes up and gives his machine a twist, and life, movement, and color unite in a razory picture, and at once he remembered his wife and his children and the venerable 1969 Oldsmobile he had driven to the discount store. Etienne LeBlanc gave a little cry, stood up, and looked around at the alien yard and the squat house with the curling roof shingles, remembering everything that ever happened to him in a shoveled-apart sequence" (152–53).

It is a bittersweet moment, for with the truth about his identity comes the realization of his situation: he has been kidnapped and forced into hard labor that is not good for his now-remembered high blood pressure. He goes inside to find his blood pressure medicine in the pants he had been wearing the day before, and looking around again, he "wonder[s] what kind of people owned no images of their kin" (153). Back outside Etienne considers knocking Andy out with the shovel, but again he is who he is, and he is apparently the kind of man who can pity Andy, who is also who he is: "Here was a criminal, though not an able or very smart one, and such people generally took the heaviest blows of life" (154). Indeed Etienne notices that Andy's "strange nose" had apparently "been broken before birth," suggesting that the violence of his life began as early as the womb (155). So instead of ending his abductor's life with a similar act of violence, Etienne finishes the ditch, waking Andy up before he makes the last cut so that he can watch the water flow.

After another night, perhaps even more frightening now that Etienne knows he is not this man's son and thus that Andy is not just lazy but also criminal, Etienne wakes up before daylight to

Andy telling him they are going for a ride and wondering what the old man can remember. Etienne continues the charade of confusion, hoping it will set Andy's mind at ease and that the ride they take will just be back into town. On the way, though, they meet up with Andy's wife, who quickly figures out what has been going on and, ironically, beats Andy with a shovel and then slaps him "like a gangster in a cheap movie" until the old man stops her, asking, again with his forthright, self-assured sense of morality, "What's wrong with you?" (158). There is no saving this couple, however, so when Andy knocks his wife down with the shovel, Etienne escapes in her truck while they are both overcome by their altercation.

The story comes to a surprisingly happy ending, though again bittersweet, after this violent climax. Arriving in the Wal-Mart parking lot, Etienne finds a young man sleeping in a car next to his own Buick, apparently hoping, even after two days and nights, that his grandfather will find his way back. And Etienne has, in more ways than one. Leaning into the car, Etienne "studied his [grandson's] face, saw the LeBlanc nose, reached in at last and traced the round-topped ears of his wife. He knew him, and his mind closed like a fist on this grandson and everything else, even his wife fading in his arms, even the stunned scowl of the copper-haired woman as she was hammered into the gravel. As if memory could be a decision, he accepted it all, knowing now that the only thing worse than reliving nightmares until the day he died was enduring a life full of strangers. He closed his eyes and called on the old farm in his head to stay where it was, remembered its cypress house, its flat and misty lake of sugar-cane keeping the impressions of a morning wind" (159).

Gautreaux is careful in this passage not to suggest that Etienne is "cured," but his use of Alzheimer's symptoms in this story is a means toward exploring the value of memories, good and bad. While this period of forgetfulness may have provided Etienne with an escape from the sad memory of the sudden loss of his wife, he has ultimately realized that forgetting his pain is not a blessing. As a man like Etienne, with his strong moral sense, knows (and as the Aldridge brothers will learn in the next novel), one better appreciates the good through experience with the bad. Just as there is "sorry blood" among and within us, so too is there "good blood." Life is full of such dichotomies. And just as Etienne was willing to accept being Ted with the attitude that "I am where I am," he seems ready now to live among his family, even without his beloved wife, for at least as long as he can remember.

"Sunset in Heaven"

> The world's full of people who don't know what year it is.
> . . . Richest woman in town and all she could appreciate was cheap food and soap operas. (170–71)

Gautreaux explores Alzheimer's more directly in "Sunset in Heaven" (the disease never having been specifically mentioned in "Sorry Blood"). Hypochondriac Chad Felder meets Alzheimer's sufferer Joe Santangelo when the latter wanders up to the former's property on a bush hog one morning. This chance encounter ultimately shows Chad that there are worse things than the possibility of catching some rare disease and dying young, but upon first seeing Joe, he thinks about how he "liked old people because they were living proof that he could steer around all the horrible diseases in life and last a good while" (162). While Joe is pondering the mystery of when "all these fancy houses" were developed, Chad considers that "here was a chance to study a survivor" (163). But the reader soon wonders if one can really term this man a survivor.

The story's placement, like the placement of "License to Steal" after "Little Frogs in a Ditch" in the previous collection, reminds the reader that there is a craft in a collection's construction. Joe is a retired farmer, like Etienne LeBlanc, and, given his advanced Alzheimer's, if not for his different name, the reader might assume that this story is picking up some years after the previous one left off, like the similar characters with different names one finds in Hemingway's *In Our Time*. So the collection, or perhaps both collections, might be considered a version of the story cycle, with their recurrent character types and similar themes and conflicts echoed throughout. Yet the stories do not repeat themselves. We left Etienne gazing upon a grandson so concerned about him that the grandson had apparently spent a night (perhaps two) in a parking lot. Joe Santangelo's daughter has not gone in search of her missing father and is also not sorry to hear of his death at the end of the story, although she truthfully corrects Chad's impression when he asks, "You didn't love him?" (174): "I didn't say that. . . . Now answer me. Did I say that?" (175).

What seems to Chad an unfeeling response to news of her father's death is merely a woman who has already learned one of the lessons Chad needs to derive from this experience. As she tells him, "You don't live forever." (175). Her father was eighty-nine and his mind was gone; why grieve over the release of his body? But Chad thought he was going to find in Joe's "life story" that the old man had "left something behind for him. Some clue, maybe, of why he rode the planet for eighty-nine years and then wound up in [Chad's] backyard" (175). And indeed, this is exactly what Joe has, accidentally of course, done.

First, upon realizing Joe's condition, Chad recognized the irony "that the old man had lived through life's accidents and diseases," which Chad fears so much, "only to wind up with Alzheimer's" (164), a diagnosis that is confirmed by Joe's former neighbor when Chad goes to where Joe had said he came from (though he hadn't lived there for quite some time, Chad learns). The neighbor, like Joe's daughter, is oddly unconcerned, or at least not panicked by the situation. He had seen Joe earlier, and Joe had "talk[ed] to [him] like it was thirty years ago" (167), so the neighbor gave Joe some gas for an old tractor still on the Santangelo property and then went on with his own day, accepting Joe's condition. As he tells Chad, "That wasn't Joe Santangelo what come by here. That was just his old body. . . . Kind of like a movin' picture, but not the real thing," the imagery echoing the movie projector imagery used in the previous story as Etienne's memory returned. Another one of the day's lessons comes from this neighbor as well, who explains Joe's behavior as "doin' things the second time in his head" (168) then says to Chad, "Mister, you can't do nothing the second time. It's the first time what count" (169).

With a clearer understanding of the situation, Chad returns home to find that Joe, whom he had left napping, has ridden off on his tractor. So he and a deputy sheriff go in pursuit, which is not an unusual assignment for the deputy; nor is it one that the deputy complains about. He is another man who apparently lives in the moment and is not unduly upset over what is out of his control. The two men find Joe—or rather, "a rag doll likeness of him" (171)—dead from a broken neck. Though it is no surprise that such an accident might occur to an old man driving a tractor through a thick wood, Chad is overcome with nausea and dizziness, and he confesses, "I'm always thinking something like this might happen to me." The deputy is perplexed by the idea of an accountant, who would have no reason to be in this kind of situation, fearing such an accident: "Why would you think that?" (172). Why, indeed—another lesson for Chad.

But Chad has yet to discern all the lessons in this odd day, so the next day he visits the old man's daughter, seeking some kind of closure, it seems. She is more concerned about the cost of the burial than the death of her father, but after she establishes that the absence of regret does not reflect a lack of love, she shares with Chad a view of heaven that he might find comforting when he worries about dying—a heaven where we do well what we enjoy doing here on earth. She asks Chad what he thinks her father is doing in heaven. Chad responds, "Farming. That's what he liked most, wasn't it?" She then asks what Chad will do there: "I guess I'd keep records for the place. . . . I'm an accountant. I like to make numbers balance out." She responds, "That's it, then. . . . That's what people want to do when they go to heaven. Their jobs. They want to get 'em right" (176). Considering what Joe's former neighbor had said about not getting second chances during this lifetime, this idea should offer comfort, in spite of Chad's seemingly mundane interests—mundane for some perhaps, but not for Chad: "He thought about what it would be like to complete an important balance sheet without his usual fear of causing a fiscal disaster. . . . Chad closed his eyes for a moment, imagining a mountain-sized computer monitor gradually lighting up at sunset [hence the story's title], its screen covered with rows of amber numerals winking like stars. He walked along the bottom of his columns, which ran as high as night itself, knowing he'd never make a mistake, never be out of balance" (177). Each man's heaven is his own.

The story ends on a light tone when the woman tries to sell Chad the tractor her father left in the woods behind Chad's property. "You can go to raising snap beans," she suggests. Then she laughs when Chad says he prefers his beans "from a can," a complaint her father, a farmer, had shared with Chad about her (177). They have chosen lives different from Joe Santangelo's, and if Chad can now enjoy his life and quit waiting for something bad to happen, it won't matter so much whether he lives another five or fifty years. The point is to live it well.

"Rodeo Parole"

> Little Claude, an accordionist who had burned down his wife's lover's house, nodded agreement. "Don't look at that judge; don't look at that bull," he said, spreading his palms out on the plywood. The fourth was a new man, a murderer who would never get out, not even after death, for no family would claim him, and someday he would be buried in the prison graveyard by the swamp. (180)

Gautreaux continues to explore quality of life as a theme in "Rodeo Parole," which takes place in a Louisiana prison. The story begins as four inmates sit at a "neon-orange card table" waiting for the bull to be let loose. The goal of this "rodeo" event is to be the team who sits at the table longest as the bull charges so as to win and thus get their pictures in the newspaper, "where the parole board would see what good Joes they were, brave competitors, winners" (179). Three of the men wonder, therefore, why the fourth has volunteered for this dangerous, indeed life-threatening, event, since he is a murderer with no opportunity for parole. He merely answers their query with "I can get out" (181). And he does: he is killed by the bull.

The story is narrated in the third person, but primarily from Jimmy's point of view. A simple burglar, Jimmy is a likely candidate for an early parole, so he has volunteered to risk his life for the positive attention his fellow inmates assure him will come to the winning team. After watching the previous foursome, he has misgivings, but he has also watched what to do, so he "will[s himself] to be like them, draining himself of feeling" as he hears the animal released. This beast is not so different from the prisoners; to fire him up for the event, the rodeo officials have stuck him with likely the same electric prods they might use to break up a prison brawl or stun an unruly inmate. Significantly, as the bull charges the orange table and four men, Gautreaux notes his "shadowed black eyes, a lurching hump on his back and, under him, his tortured, swinging bag loaded with electricity" (181). This beast of burden is not so far removed from the prisoners waiting for him to serve as their judge.

Noticing Little Claude close his eyes and "Nookey's face go blank," Jimmy misreads the murderer's contrasting widened eyes and tries to soothe him with a calming "Easy" (181), but the murderer's echoing "'Easy,' . . . with no inflection" (182) is a mere statement, one realizes upon a rereading of the story—as in "This is easy." With his sentence of more than three hundred years, the murderer has nothing to lose at this game but a lifeless life, unlike these others, who might be paroled—sooner rather than later if they "win." Though the reader may not, on first reading, realize the significance of the murderer's "easy" response, the story does settle into slow motion, allowing time in the first reading for us, along with Jimmy, to observe the murderer's appearance and to note its similarity to a sacred statue. However, none of the other men, it occurs to Jimmy, have "thought any of this," for they have apparently been successful at "drain[ing] themselves of feeling and were white and empty" (182).

The bull's attack is "directed at something it sought without knowing why, choosing the table and the men as a target with the logic a thunderbolt uses to select a tree or a house or a man walking along with a rake hoisted on his shoulder" (182). Their judge, an angel of death, seems to act randomly, neither discriminating nor distinguishing between potential victims. It wounds three of the four team members, leaving the murderer "sitting untouched in front of nothing, his hands still out flat, palms down, in the center of the ring, his hair flawless, his eyes [still] open." So while the clowns are dragging the wounded off the field and before they can go back to distract the bull, it charges one last time "like a train." While the burglar Jimmy, who only suffers having the wind knocked out of him, "*rob[s]* his share of the atmosphere in little sips until he could breathe again" (emphasis added), he watches the murderer's body dragged off the field. When Jimmy is told that another team has won and there can only be "one winner," he responds, "Maybe so" (183). Like Joe Santangelo's daughter, Jimmy apparently believes that the murderer is better off dead—indeed, that seems to have been the man's plan and thus, in a sense, he has won the rodeo.

"Dancing with the One-Armed Gal"

> He listened to her through the meal and decided that he'd rather spend eight hours a day with his tongue stuck on a hot pipe than teach in a college. (193)

Welding with Children ends with another unlikely hero who rescues a woman from herself. At the start of "Dancing with the One-Armed Gal" Iry Boudreaux is lost in a cowboy novel when the compressor he is supposed to be monitoring blows up. His girlfriend, Babette, who is also his boss, fires him, saying, "You need a vacation [to g]et your head out of those books [and g]o look at some real stuff" (187). The next morning, Iry goes to

Mass, where he contemplates his relationship, knowing that his behavior puzzles Babette, and wonders if he is good at anything. Iry "suddenly felt inauthentic, as though he no longer owned a real position in his little town," so he "headed west toward Texas," apparently to find out who he is, as opposed to who he has been pretending to be (188).

Iry doesn't get far before he meets up with the title character of this story, who is hitchhiking home to Texas after also being fired. As they drive along together, the two find, to their surprise, that they have more in common than losing their jobs, but this is not a love story. By story's end Iry is going back to Louisiana to reconnect with Babette, this time with a stronger sense of self, which he achieves while trying to encourage the hitchhiker to present herself more authentically as well. Thus does another blue-collar worker come to the aid of a woman, who in this case resists his help at first, having self-identified as a lesbian feminist who should not need rescue by a member of the patriarchy.

Claudine Glover is understandably wary at first of taking a ride from a man, but her car has broken down, and he seems friendly and harmless, so she accepts a ride. Like most hitchhikers in Iry's experience, Claudine tells him her life story as they ride along: "Iry guessed people thought they owed you an explanation when you helped them out" (190). Claudine reports that she has been fired from a college teaching position, and when Iry notes that he has lost his job, too, she remarks that her situation is still more dire, academic appointments being fewer than blue-collar jobs: "I am a professor of women's studies. . . . It took me a long time to get that position, and now after four years of teaching, I lost it. . . . You don't know how it is in academics. My Ph.D. is not from the best institution. You've got to find your little niche and hold on, because if you don't get tenure, you're pretty much done for" (190–91). This then is another of Gautreaux's stories of academics, of the smaller world he spent so many years in within his home state of Louisiana. This one, with elements reminiscent of Richard Russo's 1997 *Straight Man*, candidly criticizes academics' tendency to reinvent themselves for job security. Ironically academia ultimately offers the most secure jobs, after tenure, but by that time the academic has often forgotten who she was before identifying herself into that niche. The academic reader may find Claudine sympathetic and also may find him- or herself envying Iry.

It is a long drive to El Paso, Texas, plenty of time for Iry to figure out, if not what women's studies is exactly, at least that Claudine has not been honest about who she is, not only to him but also to her previous employers. In her desperation to keep her job, Claudine has convinced herself that her job security is tied up with how she contributes to her small college meeting certain quotas. Believing she got the job based upon her gender and feeling her position threatened by the college's opportunity to hire an African American, she claimed to be one-sixteenth African American. Then when other women's studies professors are hired, she plays up her physical handicap by no longer wearing her prosthesis; and finally she comes out as a lesbian. When Iry asks her, "Ain't you no good at teaching studying women?" (192), she admits that her students do like her and her scholarship is published, so Iry ultimately guesses what her employer guessed: that she is not black and may not be a lesbian. Thus in spite of the stories Claudine tells that are so foreign to Iry's experience—"university politics, glass ceilings" (193)—ultimately, Iry realizes, she was fired for a reason anyone can understand—dishonesty. She is more inauthentic than Iry was feeling when he left home, so being around her and witnessing true unawareness of self brings back his own self-confidence in who he is. He then turns his attention to helping her to recognize her true identity.

But first Claudine tries to disillusion Iry regarding his romantic notions of the West. Having grown up on a ranch and dreading going back to it, she responds to the idea of Iry heading west on vacation to see the places he reads about in westerns by telling him about raising cows to kill them, about getting lost out on her own land and feeling so small and insignificant in so much space, and about losing her arm in a horseback riding accident. Reflecting how his romanticism is part of his positive nature, Iry merely determines from her efforts to deromanticize the West with these stories that she was "born unhappy, like his cousin Ted, who'd won $92,000 in the lottery and yet had to be medicated when he found out about the tax due on his winnings" (194–95). In other words her "weird man-hating" studies might have contributed to her cynicism, but Gautreaux does not ultimately blame academics for her perpetual bad humor; she was already "warp[ed]," though maybe this is a comment on the type of people drawn to academics, a place that casts people into such narrow niches that they feel less "like a speck of dust" in the big, wide world (194).

Refusing to be similarly warped by Claudine's negative viewpoint, Iry stops at a cowboy museum along the way, continuing on his own agenda even as he accommodates hers. He examines the museum's artifacts "as though he were in the Louvre," while she finds that the place "feels like a tomb" (195). He compares cowboys to Neil Armstrong; she perceives them as a "vestige of obsolete paternalistic culture." When she points out the absence of "images of women" in the museum, he counters with what she views as an inaccurate cliché: that the "romance of isolation," as she terms it, would not work for women, who "are more family—that is, social-like. They're people people." She considers this to be generalizing, but he then supports his thesis with the two of them: "I'm heading off into the brush to look at stuff, not people, stuff. You going home to stay with Mama." Gautreaux ends this section of the story with "He expected a scowl, but she looked at him closely, as though he had suddenly revealed another identity to her" (196). Most likely she had been stereotyping him, too, and has now realized that his blue-collar occupation does not reflect his intelligence as she might have expected.

At the next stop, then, the place "where Judge Roy Bean had presided," Claudine uses Iry's own metaphor for this man's accomplishment: "Now, I've got to concede that here's a real astronaut. . . . A wild man comes where there is no law and just says, 'I am the law.' . . . He staked out his territory." Then Iry continues to surprise Claudine with his grasp of her situation, which she thought he couldn't understand: "Ain't that what professors do? . . . You say I'm going to be the Tillie Dogschmidt scholar. She's my territory because I'm the first to read all her poems or whatever and study what all everybody's written about her. That what you called 'carving your niche,' right? Some kind of space you claim, just like the judge here did?" (197). She thinks he is "belittl[ing]" what she does, but he says otherwise: "I think it's great. You invent yourself a job out of thin air. Wish I could do that" (197–98). She is hurt, still thinking he is making fun of her, but when she asks, "Am I just not a real person to you?" he counters, "Am I to you?" (198). He realizes they are each figuring out the other; having cast him as a particular type, she thinks he has done the same to her.

The next lesson Iry starts to impart is the big one for all philosophers (she does, after all, have a Ph.D.): *Know thyself.* He asks her if she has any job prospects in El Paso, and she tells him of one possibility: "Mom knows the head of the English Department at a community college in the desert. I just have to show up and sell myself. . . . Tell them how rare a bird I am. How I'll fill all their quotas in one shot. . . . I'm a crippled black woman and a gay feminist" (198–99). Iry suggests, rather, "Just tell them you're a good teacher" (199). The job talk depresses her, and she gets drunk during dinner, adding alcohol to antidepressants. Iry tries to call it a night, but then he asks her to dance when he sees how low she is feeling. And during this dance, he realizes that she is lying about herself. First, he determines that she is straight, based on her response to dancing with him—"I'm not being a very good lesbian"—and that she "dance[s] backward too good" to be a lesbian; in addition he notes that she doesn't move like a black woman (202). Claudine calls him on his generalizations, and perhaps he is drawing on his own limited worldview, but in this case he is apparently not wrong. When she shows him family pictures, he recognizes her mother's Italian, not African, heritage: "Grand Crapaud has more Italians than Palermo. I went to Catholic school with a hundred of them. This lady looks like a Cefalue." When Claudine still insists, he asks, "When I bring you home tomorrow, can I ask her?" to which Claudine "hissed, 'Don't you dare.'" So Iry finally says to Claudine, "Now I know why you really got your butt fired. . . . You lied to those people at the college. And they knew it. I mean, if I can figure you out in a couple days, don't you think they could after a few years?" (203). While she lashes out in anger, he calmly and graciously identifies her to herself: "You're a straight white woman who's a good teacher because she loves what she's doing." Still she insists upon her own self-identification—"I'm a gay African-American who was crippled by a horse"—but he counters,

"You're crippled all right, but the horse didn't have nothin' to do with it" (204).

Somewhat to his surprise Claudine is still there the next morning, waiting for a ride the rest of the way home. Upon arriving, Iry invites himself in with the little white lie to Claudine's mother by which he tests his theory of her true ethnicity, "Your daughter told me you make some great pasta sauce" (204–5). After lunch and before leaving, Iry tries one last time to help Claudine let go of her handicap. This time though, he almost goes too far when he tries to get her to forgive horses for her physical injury, reminding her that only one horse hurt her and that she has since generalized about all horses: "You don't like [this horse] because of something his millionth cousin did" (206). But Claudine is truly frightened when Iry brings her too close to the animal, and Iry leaves her crying in her mother's arms. Feeling bad for causing her further unhappiness, Iry calls a couple of days later to find out about the job—which she did not get, simply because, she admits, "there weren't any vacancies at the moment" (207). Baby steps for Claudine, the reader realizes, but she is at least not creating a political excuse for this outcome.

But Iry, recognizing how "inauthentic" some people are, is feeling better about himself, and when he calls home to Louisiana, Babette tells him that he was not at fault for the compressor accident after all. She asks him to come back to work and, presumably, back to her, but he says that he needs first "to see a little more of this country. . . . I can't figure it out yet" (207). He tells Babette about meeting "this one-armed gal [who] hates it out here," which he can't understand: "It's pretty out here, and she don't want nothing to do with it," preferring to be in New Orleans. Babette remarks that people out West come

East "to see stuff" (208). There are tourists everywhere, people, the story seems to say, who leave home to figure out who they are—like Claudine and Iry (and like Colette in *The Next Step in the Dance*). With food for thought, he hangs up and then, eavesdropping on an Indian using a pay phone in the hope of hearing him speak Navajo but hearing instead a question about what kind of milk to buy and then noticing that a necklace he just bought for Babette was "Made in India" (so it *was* made by *Indians*, as the shop girl told him), Iry determines it is time to go home after all. He now feels, in contrast to all the deception around him, "authentic beyond belief" (209).

As a writer Gautreaux is concerned with authenticity. Critics praise his ability to write realistic dialogue, but one should also recognize a "realism" in his stories' happy endings. Talking about the dark themes in contemporary literature, Gautreaux acknowledges that many people do get away with their bad behavior and "such stories belong in the canon. But the mistake a writer of those types of stories makes, I think, is to write *all* of his stories like that because then, cumulatively, the author gets away from realism." Sometimes people do come out of bad situations having learned something and evolved, as in most of the stories of *Welding with Children*. The danger in writing stories in which people succeed, of course, is of slipping into sentimentality. Success stories, he says, are "hard as hell to write without making them seem simple-minded or clichéd or insipid or sentimental. The most frightening thing in the world to an intelligent writer is sentimentality. He doesn't want a molecule of it in his fiction. But I think if you read enough and you understand how to blend humor and irony and the right tone in with the bad stuff, you can write a story that carries an emotional load yet is not sentimental in the least" (Bauer, "Interview").

After writing two volumes of short stories and a novel where most often the good guys win and the bad guys get punished—giving readers a welcome respite from the darker fiction of his contemporaries—Gautreaux turned to "concerns that were a bit more thematically sober" in his next book.[12] As he sends his characters deep into the Louisiana swamp in the next two novels, he explores, Hawthorne-like, the depths of the psyche that sometimes mirrors the savage settings. But still his heroes will resist their baser drives and ultimately thrive, while his villains are ultimately punished, if only by simply being themselves.

CHAPTER 5

The Clearing

> He wondered if the many-fanged geography rubbed off
> on people, made them primal, predatory. Had it changed
> him? Why else would he be out on this errand, risking
> gunfire? What had affected him if not the land itself that
> sickened and drowned his workers, land that would eat
> him alive, too, if given half a chance.

Gautreaux's second novel, *The Clearing*, is set just after World
War I in Louisiana, though its two main characters are from Pennsylvania. So this is not only a historical novel, but it also echoes
an early southern literary tradition in Gautreaux's employment
of a naive Yankee outsider (the younger of the two Pittsburgh
brothers) coming south and observing from his presumed intellectually and morally superior perspective the customs and conditions of this supposedly less civilized part of the country. Also
harkening back to this nineteenth-century southern literary tradition, the novel is set shortly after the country has been at war,
though in this case it is World War I rather than the Civil War, and
the brothers to be reunited in this novel were not divided by
loyalties to opposite sides of the war between the states but brothers who have been separated since the elder succumbed to their
father's urging and enlisted in the service to fight in Europe.

The story reaches back even further than nineteenth-century
literary traditions, to the biblical traditions that have long informed southern literature and culture. In the novel are echoes
of the various New Testament parables—of the prodigal son and

the lost sheep, and of the wasted talents—as well as Old Testament stories of brother pitted against brother, although Gautreaux's two brothers deeply love each other and there is little rivalry between them.

The novel also reflects the contemporary sensibilities of other recent historical novels, reminding readers of novels such as Charles Frazier's *Cold Mountain* that explore the postwar experience of veterans—whatever the war—from the perspective of the present-day author who writes with an informed awareness of conditions such as posttraumatic stress disorder. Gautreaux recalls an uncle who suffered shellshock after his World War I experience, from whom the writer came to understand that "everybody that gets involved in the business of shooting people with rifles is damaged and changed." When asked if his World War I novels were also inspired by the current and previous Gulf Wars, Gautreaux responded, "When someone writes a novel thirty or forty years from now, there's going to be a war going on somewhere and the same question is going to be asked: 'Are you thinking about this present war?' There's always a present war, it seems. The fact that it's going on while I'm writing a novel about psychologically damaged warriors, that's just the way it happens. In a way, all wars are the same war."[1]

Though *The Clearing*'s Byron Aldridge survived the war, he does not settle into his role as heir apparent upon his return home. Angry with his father for encouraging him into the experience that continues to haunt him, Byron extends his military service into a vocation in law enforcement, and after a brief stint on the Pittsburgh police force, which outrages his father, he leaves Pennsylvania for Indiana, then moves to Missouri, Arkansas, Kansas, New Mexico, and finally Louisiana. Once Byron is discovered to be in Louisiana, Mr. Aldridge buys the lumber mill where Byron serves as constable and sends his younger son Randolph to run the mill, as well as to reconnect with, rehabilitate, and recruit his brother to resume the older son's rightful place as the head of the business when their father retires.

While Byron's choice to be constable in a timber community suggests that he must *want* his family to find him—or at least is drawn to the *familiar* on some level, his family having long been in the lumber business—he does not want to return to the fold. Neither, however, does he reject the idea of renewing his relationship with his innocent, naive younger brother, perhaps as a way of reconnecting with his own prewar, uncorrupted self.[2] But the inherent violence underneath the veneer of civilization (symbolized by such art forms as music, which plays a key role in the novel)—or just outside of it, whether in the jungles of the Congo (the novel's setup being somewhat reminiscent of Conrad's *Heart of Darkness*) or the swamps of Louisiana—is a lesson all men eventually learn, sometimes in trial by the weapon fire of war but also in times of so-called peace, when an alligator can rise up out of the swamp and snatch a mill worker from the shore as easily as an argument can erupt during a poker game and end with one man shooting another. Following his brother into the swamps of Louisiana, Gautreaux's "heart of darkness," Randolph becomes Marlowe to Byron's Kurtz.[3] Significantly, during one night of his journey, as the steamboat "struggled along a bayou as narrow as a ditch" deeper into the swamp, Randolph sees "something like a longhaired wolf" coming at him over the rail. It is merely a "moss-eaten limb" that "retreat[s] like a monster's claw," but the nightmarish imagery reflects a childlike quality to Randolph's state of mind as he "voyage[s] beyond the things he knew" to find his older brother. Later, in his bunk, Randolph thinks about Byron, "a good swimmer who never feared the water, not even at night, and he fell asleep remembering the time he learned to float on his back, Byron's fingertips training the bones in his spine to drift level and rise toward the air" (23). Byron taught him to float, presumably to swim, and now Byron will teach him about life and death, good and evil, and the love that makes the suffering worth living through.

Reviews of Gautreaux's books often include praise for the credibility of his character development and the authenticity of his dialogue, and when he is asked about these elements, the author attributes his success to writing about the people he knows, the voices he hears all around him in his native state. So it was quite a chance the writer took to put two "Yankees" at the center of this story. Gautreaux believes, however, that these characters help to broaden his novel's audience: "Folks who are not from the deep South can read *The Clearing* and experience the region better because they're seeing it through eyes like theirs, eyes of outsiders who struggle to cope with the climate, attitudes, traditions, reptiles and everything else" (Fitten, 108). And certainly there are still plenty of Louisiana voices in the novel to supply the authentic banter, the numerous different accents and dialects one can hear in Gautreaux's anything-but-homogenous home state. As in Gautreaux's story "Died and Gone to Vegas," in this novel a variety of ethnicities and cultures are represented within a single Louisiana community: Cajun, Creole, Italian, African American, and, with the addition of the two Pennsylvania brothers, Yankee Protestant. One is reminded of Mark Twain's *Adventures of Huckleberry Finn*, in which Twain employed numerous distinct southern dialects as Huck and Jim traveled up and down the Mississippi. Gautreaux's work reflects the variety of voices one might hear traveling from one end of a Louisiana parish to the other.[4]

Also reminiscent of Twain, particularly his early California stories in which a local yokel tells a story to a more educated, supposedly intellectually superior easterner, Gautreaux inserts into his novel the Aldridge brothers, particularly new arrival Randolph, to *hear* and note the unusual presence of so many different voices. In an interview with Robert Birnbaum, Gautreaux comments upon one reason for this choice of outsider protagonists—to help himself avoid a southern novel cliché in which one finds "a bunch of uneducated deplorable folks [who] self-destruct for four hundred pages." What the "outlander" perspective accomplishes, furthermore, he notes, is "a different chemistry": "You put the non-Southern reader into the novel with this particular choice that I made. It seems like a simple choice, but it has had a profound effect on how people take the action that goes on in the book. It's not just a bunch of depraved people beating up on each other. It's some sensitive people, some Yankees, my god, who are down there."[5] In *The Clearing* he reminds us that depravity is not a uniquely southern, Cajun, or hillbilly characteristic but that, as the Puritans believed, given the right circumstances it is a natural inclination of human beings in their struggle for survival—as Randolph Aldridge discovers in the course of the novel.

Another element of credibility in Gautreaux's characterization is his characters' moral sensibilities. None of these people are all good, and not even the villains are all bad. L. Lamar Nisly has argued that the "chief villain behind all of the particular villains" in the novel is "war,"[6] the violence of which has corrupted not only Byron's psyche but also the less sympathetic characters Buzetti and Crouch, whose violent behavior is related to Buzetti having seen his three brothers bayoneted in one day's battles and to Crouch having been tortured and forced to kill wounded

Italian soldiers while held as a prisoner of war.[7] As Arthur Miller shows in *Playing for Time* that the real horror about the chief guard of the concentration camp is that she is human and not some kind of monster, so too does Gautreaux, with these details about his two most reprehensible characters, remind us that they are human beings whose villainy has arisen from their own suffering. That is not to defend their violent acts directed against people who played no part in their personal losses, but rather to flesh out even the villains in the novel. "There is nothing so unreal or boring as an entirely evil fictional character," Gautreaux has asserted. "You cannot write about even despicable characters as though they are one-dimensional or entirely evil. There has got to be something that makes the reader see in them something positive or admirable or at least worthy of sympathy" (Levasseur and Rabalais, 37).

Gautreaux made this observation in response to a question about his story "License to Steal," in which, as the two interviewers note, Louisiana is seen as separate from the rest of the country (Levasseur and Rabalais, 37); the reader may recall that Curtis's wife "was tired of living in Louisiana [and] wanted to move to the United States."[8] This attitude anticipates Randolph's reaction to Louisiana in *The Clearing*, and the author's reference to the sympathetic appeal that one of his students found in the story's main character, Curtis, anticipates the characterization of Buzetti and Crouch in *The Clearing*. What makes this novel less negative than the lighter-toned "License to Steal" (which Gautreaux called in this 1999 interview, his "most negative" to date) is the exploration in the novel of what has sent Buzetti and Crouch, and Byron and Randolph, down the path of violence. We don't have as much to go on to tell us why Curtis is such a loser, but we quickly grasp the reason Byron seems compelled to chase his long-suffering wife away (though in contrast to Curtis's wife, Byron's seems intent upon staying).

Like Frazier's Inman in *Cold Mountain*, Byron feels corrupted beyond redemption by what he witnessed during the war. He first went to France as a civilian, "observing" for a powder company to guide expansion and production decisions based on what was happening on the front. The U.S. government then hired him to give intelligence reports on his observations, which also influenced his letters home to his family, in which he would vacillate between descriptions of the beautiful cathedrals and countrysides, as though sending vacation postcards, and reporting on seeing boxcars and fields full of soldiers' bodies. And after all that witnessing, when he wanted to come home, he instead did as his father urged and joined up, thus becoming part of the destruction he had to that point only observed: "Watching, I found out, is nothing like being in battle," he tells Randolph (101). In a scene reminiscent of the final battle in Twain's *Connecticut Yankee in King Arthur's Court*—Twain recognizing that war is timeless, that what changes is the kind of weapons we use, and that progress ultimately means better weapons—Byron realizes that the "first wave was *supposed* to get shot and tangled in the wire" so that their bodies could be used as stepping stones for the next wave to cross over, and in that insight he learns "the worth of one life to a damned general" (103).[9]

Upon finally returning to the states, Byron found himself, like other members of the Lost Generation, unable to just settle back, as if nothing has happened, into the upper-middle-class life his father wants him to resume. (The novel thus also echoes Hemingway's post–World War I fiction.) Perhaps Byron's decision to go into law enforcement is an attempt to insure against witnessing that kind of mass destruction on his own native soil; as he tells Randolph, "I just bang around from badge to badge trying to make fellows do right" (41), and, as he tells his wife, "When I'm going up against a real bastard, I just feel the rightness of it" (89). Randolph is appalled by Byron's paradoxically violent peacekeeping methods. In contrast to his brother, "Randolph had heard a great deal about suffering but had experienced none of it and discounted even his father's tales of his own hard youth" (10). So while Byron may be trying, in reestablishing a relationship with his brother, to reconnect with his own more innocent youth, Randolph will, in his brother's new community in Louisiana, witness and ultimately experience the violence and corruption that haunt Byron.

Randolph is the less tortured brother to Byron's prodigal son, and he is less interesting at the start for his acceptance of status quo, his industrialist/capitalist mentality. He does not even allow himself to resent his father's determination to bring Byron back to Pittsburgh to resume his rightful place as head of the business, even though it is Randolph who has dutifully and successfully managed it for his father in Byron's absence: "He took what little love his father allotted him and made do with it" (209). Nisly notes Randolph's Protestant work ethic, which lacks spiritualism (115). Randolph is essentially still a boy, an innocent, when he arrives. Married but childless, he seems to have been playing house as well as playing at mill manager, not yet having reached an adult level of understanding consequences since he has not yet experienced any significant consequences as a result of his own decisions and actions. But like Hawthorne's Young Goodman Brown and Conrad's Marlowe, Randolph enters the wilderness and will emerge a changed man who has experienced the irreversible consequences of one's choices and actions.

Traveling to Nimbus, the "clearing" (not yet quite a community) where the new mill is situated and where Byron is constable, is no easy journey after arriving by rail in New Orleans, where he is told that the trestle going into the swamp has collapsed into a bayou, requiring the next leg of his journey to be made by steamboat, which Randolph believed to be "a thing of the past" (15). Once on the steamboat, however, Randolph is "impressed by" the "efficiency" of the chief mate's "businesslike anger" behind his work orders to his men, rather than appalled by the man's dehumanizing epithets, like "Go on you crippled sows" (16). The reader learns that Randolph, raised in a supposedly civilized, upper-middle-class home, is drawn to efficiency "like the clink of a silver coin on pavement" (17), the imagery reflecting his interest in profit. How far removed is the view of men as part of an industrial machine from the military general's lack of regard for the individual soldier in his battle plan? But to be fair, the first time Randolph hears of the death of one of the mill workers, which he did not witness but rather hears about when he asks his engineer what happened to his fireman and learns, "Your brother kilt him," the industrial analogy that comes to his mind, "His dead worker had been shipped off like a faulty machine returned to the manufacturer," reflects his own surprise that "no one seemed to question what had happened" (57).

When the marshal finally shows up to question Randolph, he also explains to the young man that his brother's methods are socially acceptable: "He can pound the shit out of whatever bastard needs it." As though sensing Randolph's concern about his brother's character after hearing testimony of such violent methods of keeping order, the marshal adds, "He's a good man" (59). Several years Randolph's senior, the marshal is himself still working through the idea of killing in the name of justice, and here he introduces a central question posed by the novel: "I got a friend who's a priest. He says it's a sin to kill. I got no problem with that, but what if I don't kill one, and that one kills two or three? Did I kill that two or three? I can't figure that out. . . . I learned early on how men have to do. I didn't want to learn that, but I did" (59–60).[10] And so too must Randolph learn "how men have to do," though for a while he tries to protect himself from the difficult question of when to sanction—even participate in—violence by thinking of his mill workers as "pieces of mechanism that now and again failed, only to be discarded and replaced. He was the chief gear in the machine, where the motion started, and he was not supposed to worry about who was broken or stripped down the line" (140).[11] Indeed, when the doctor gives up on one shooting victim past saving, Randolph urges him to try, saying, "My God, he's our engineer" (123).

This man is shot after Randolph persuaded Byron to put down his gun and "try and handle it some other way." Byron, who associates himself with "the angel of death" (who is, he tells his younger brother, "still an angel"), continues to wield a weapon on his rounds, swinging the large shovel to knock out the instigators when he saw trouble brewing (105). When the death count continues in spite of this "other way" of handling the bar fights, Randolph then tries to encourage his brother to "shoot to wound. If they die anyway, you'll still have tried to do right"—not yet accepting that "right" might mean killing someone, as the marshal had suggested, since it may stop this man from taking more victims. Still naive, Randolph does not see the contradiction in the advice he gives: "Just do what has to be done. But try not to kill anyone" (126). Ironically, though, it is Byron, not Randolph, who ends this scene crying over the most recently killed man (whom he might have saved if he had been using a gun) as he tells of having to call the man's family in Houston. But it is not long after this incident that Randolph is compelled to pick up a firearm and shoot a man to protect both himself and another, and with this killing, in self-defense though it may have been, he comes to a clearer understanding of his brother's ghosts. He too feels corrupted by the blood on his hands and wonders how his wife will look at him once she knows he has killed.

Lillian, Randolph's wife, has joined him in Louisiana by the time that Randolph is having Byron change his methods of dealing with the saloon brawls. Upon her arrival Lillian tells her husband that she has done some growing up herself in his absence (117). Thinking of her early in the novel, Randolph had noted that she "could not function living alone" (104–5), but then she journeys to Nimbus, which Randolph knows from experience is not an easy accomplishment. He credits her energy, so different from "the subdued state she'd sunk down into over the past few years" to "the trip to this place" and is "reminded of how strange and foreign this country truly was" (118). Lillian also is going into the forest, as Hawthorne's Faith did on the same night as her husband, Young Goodman Brown. Lillian's plan is to live in nearby Tiger Island (the setting for Gautreaux's first novel), which offers more "civilized" quarters than Nimbus, but since the Aldridge brothers have tangled with the mob by this time, she is not safe there and settles in New Orleans, which as a city is considered less vulnerable to the clandestine violence of the mob hit men, particularly the one-eyed Crouch, who has been hired to kill Byron. But after some time in New Orleans, Lillian moves to Nimbus so that she and Randolph may more regularly engage in sexual relations and thus, they hope, finally conceive a child.

The seeming infertility of both of the Aldridge marriages is interesting. Ella has lived with Byron the whole time they have been married, and they have not conceived a child. Lillian and Randolph tried unsuccessfully for six years prior to Randolph's departure for Louisiana. May, Randolph's mixed-race house-keeper, in contrast, conceives easily, slipping one night into bed with Randolph and initiating relations while he sleeps so that consummation occurs before he is entirely awake. She has tried this once previously with Byron, after he had gotten drunk while Ella was out of town. That attempt was not fruitful, and she may have tried with other white men, but still, it is a relatively quick conception in contrast to how long Randolph and Lillian have actively but unsuccessfully endeavored to have a child.

Given the quiet background in which Ella allows Byron to keep her, as well as Lillian's absence at the beginning of the novel, May's presence is the only feminine influence in the story for quite a while. Her influence upon Randolph largely involves pushing him toward growing up. After several deaths have occurred, before being the direct cause of any, and even as he is struggling to understand Byron's depression and to persuade Byron to find less violent means of keeping order, Randolph is unconsciously drawn to Byron's escape method. Considering how Byron seeks comfort in music, hoping it will bring back the more innocent consciousness of his youth, when Randolph finds himself sleepless and depressed after witnessing the German shooting victim's death, he picks up his accordion, waking May with the music he plays. He explains this late-night disturbance—"I guess I was trying to find something redemptive in his death"—to which May responds, "You were with him when he died. . . . Tell truth. You see anything beautiful about it? Or was it just another sawmill man shot up in a poker game? . . . You all have got to deal with what is." In this case, for example, "Mr.

Hans could make those engines run like a chicken on Sunday morning, all right, but he was a nasty drunk and smelled like a lost dishrag" (128). She is not sure, apparently, that the deceased is worth the tears she witnessed from Byron the night before, the tears Randolph was about to cry when she interrupted his accordion playing, or her own lost sleep.

Besides steering Randolph away from attempting his brother's (failed) remedy for dealing with all the death and destruction he has witnessed since the war, May also introduces him to the dark, roux-based stews of Cajun cooking, symbolic of the rich culture he finds in Louisiana, and points out to him the value of his love for his brother. Explaining her choice of him to father her child, she says, "I went with you because you love your brother, that's all. And that kind of thing can come to the child." She stirs Randolph's longing for his wife but rejects him once her goal is achieved, "an all-white baby" she can take with her out of Louisiana, where they can pass and thus live beyond her prescribed fate in the Deep South, to "just have babies and starve" (113). Writing outside of the traditional tropes of passing literature, Gautreaux has May test the color of her progeny before she tries to pass (rather than fear the possibility of a baby's African features showing up should she have a baby with a white husband later on), but he works within the tropes of the traditional tragic octoroon story, in which the woman who seeks to pass and thus deny her race usually dies in the end. Thus is May employed as African American characters are often used in the fiction of white writers—as a step in the brothers' redemption, her life being an example of the kind of suffering some innocent people endure without having to go to war, and her death leaving her mixed-race son to his father and uncle, a means toward their salvation from suffering, if not her own.[12]

While he also risks employing archetypes from nineteenth-century southern writing of the sexual black woman and asexual white woman, Gautreaux's point with May's prompt pregnancy, given the failure of both white women to conceive seems, rather, to be more in line with the symbolic infertility of the corrupt white South found in modern southern literature—except, of course, that neither the Aldridge brothers nor their wives are southern, which directs the reader again to consider what other significance the couples' failure to reproduce might have.

As though one must want children to have them, Byron's psychological scarring from his war experience seems to affect his ability to conceive a child—with either his wife or May. There is no indication in the novel that he suffers any physical injury that might influence his ability to have children, and Ella is pregnant by the close of the novel. But in the fictional world of this novel, Byron's postwar perception of the irredeemably corrupt world might be associated with his childlessness. What kind of future would the modern world offer a child? Ironically, until Byron is able to see the world through the eyes of a child he believes is his, May's son, and to enjoy that world again while playing with the little boy, his wife does not conceive. While the *symbolism* of Byron's infertility may be the stuff of literary worlds, it does often happen that when a couple adopts a child, as Byron and Ella essentially do after May dies and Randolph, thinking he is dying, names Byron the father, the couple conceives, no longer pressured by the fear of infertility. As Ella predicts when they discuss the "fact" of Walter's supposed paternity, "I guess someday we might have one that's mine too. They say one like this can cause another to come on" (286). But perhaps her pregnancy is also a result of a more loving marriage, for Byron's soul is uplifted by the news that Walter is his son.

It is unfortunate that in the real world, many people conceive easily who are not yet ready to have children, but in the realm of this novel, Randolph and Lillian's childlessness can be related early on in the novel to the fact that they are simply not mature enough to be parents. As noted previously, they seem only to be playing house, and until they recognize, like Hawthorne's newly-weds in "The Maypole of Merry Mount," the harsher and darker elements of the world, until they know suffering, until they recognize the consequences of adulthood—including the fact that they can become responsible for helpless babies—they do not, thank goodness, become parents. Yet at novel's end these two remain childless (Randolph has even given up his son by May to his brother), even though their age of innocence has certainly come to an end.

Gautreaux explains that "it was a conscious choice" to leave this couple childless: "It was a big sacrifice to give up that child. I think the fact that they remain childless through the end of the novel is to demonstrate how big a sacrifice giving up Walter really was" (Bauer, "Interview"). The reader may recall Randolph's realization early in the novel that he had not experienced suffering—before coming to Louisiana, that is. His experiences in Nimbus have certainly changed that. He leaves much less innocent than he arrived: his conscience suffers when he kills a man and later leads many men into a battle with the mob that results in numerous deaths; he witnesses several other killings, including the murder of May; the baby is bitten by a snake dropped into his crib as revenge against the Aldridge brothers; Lillian is attacked, and he is shot and unable to defend her; then, thinking he is dying, he gives up his son to his brother, telling Byron, "I lied. . . . May told me. . . . He's yours" (284). This last act causes the most personal suffering, for when he survives his bullet wounds, Randolph cannot bring himself to take back the lie and thus the gift of the child, who brings such comfort to Byron's suffering soul. Before the shooting Randolph had seen his brother playing with the child, and the brothers had suffered together when Walter was bitten by a snake; when their father expresses his pleasure over learning of his grandson, Randolph observes "his brother's old grin come back" (288). Perhaps his own sacrifice, then, of his son for his brother, makes up for being the younger son and thus not the one their father pushed to enlist. Indeed, perhaps his awareness of this positive side of being the younger son has been what has allowed Randolph to deal so complacently with his father's efforts to bring Byron back and thereby to participate in efforts that would ultimately displace Randolph himself in the family business. For the author, the sacrifice reflects "how much Randolph loves his brother" (Bauer, "Interview").

Now that he has truly endured suffering and wonders about the sanctity of his own soul—"if he would be punished by God for the deaths he caused or if the killing itself was the punishment" (293)—Randolph can better understand *how* if not *what* Byron suffers, as he tries to explain to his father, who says Byron "should be all over that. . . . Many others have gone to war and come back fine." Reflecting his developing insight, Randolph responds, "There is no way anyone can tell you or me what he suffered" (210). After Randolph recovers from the worst of his own physical suffering, he realizes that he has just begun his own emotional suffering, and his deep love for his brother emerges as stronger than any selfish desires he might have. Randolph remains silent when their father recognizes the child as Byron's, even as Mr. Aldridge chastises his younger son for not reporting the news of a grandson in his letters. Randolph even keeps the secret truth to himself when Lillian says she kind of wishes her suspicions had been right and that he, rather than Byron, was the father. "Nothing pays like suffering," Byron had responded when Randolph wondered why the mob went after the child with a snake (233). And Byron has paid and paid. But the war is finally over for him, it seems, with the gift of a son. As he tells his sister-in-law after Randolph told him Walter is his, "'This is some news.' . . . He raised his face to her, smiling a *regular* smile. 'Tall headlines . . . like they used at the *end of the war*'" (285; emphasis added). It is "Good News," indeed, this gift of a son. But in Gautreaux's retelling of the New Testament story, it is both the father (Randolph) and the son (Walter) who suffer, nearly die, and are resurrected—so that the son might spread the news of a brighter future (to his surrogate father, Byron), in spite of the death and destruction of the past.[13]

A lesser writer might have opted for the neater ending, with poetic justice applied, Lillian finally expecting a baby rather than or at least along with Ella, everyone on the brink of happily ever after. But true suffering is not so short lived. It has taken years for Byron to emerge from his war experience, and fast healing is not in store for Randolph either. As he convalesces from his bullet wounds, his confinement allows Randolph plenty of time with his "nephew," ample opportunity to see his brother basking in fatherhood, his sister-in-law enjoying finally having a child with another one on the way—time, in short, to suffer and thus to understand the consequences of capitalism and industrialism, such as that villainous war that transformed Byron and Buzetti and Crouch (and so many others). The reader is assured that Randolph will not turn into his own father, as he was prone to do at the novel's opening. Considering the destruction of nature required to construct a civilization, as witnessed by Randolph and Byron as they look around at the much larger "clearing" their father's lumber mill has created, before returning to that civilization, Randolph learns that he must build something positive with the boards from those trees, like the school house his wife had him build in Nimbus to draw families to the community so that the men might not spend their off-duty hours just drinking and gambling—and killing.

Lillian too is now on the right track, but she has not earned this son or another child as the long-suffering Ella has. Lillian has only relatively recently become the helpmate of her husband (in the most positive sense of the term). Upon moving from New Orleans to live in Nimbus with Randolph, asking only that he "build [her] a bathroom"—and surprisingly, instructing him to "feed it with a cypress cistern" (153–54), reflecting, even as she does ask for a modern convenience, that she has grown enough to think about how to go about getting it. She also asks about adding a parlor, "where I could read and sew and have a little office of my own" (154), which anticipates the "civilizing" influence her presence will have on the whole community. Once living in Nimbus, she prompts Randolph to add a school and church services to the community, realizing that families are a more effective means of keeping the men out of drunken brawls than closing down the saloons. More quickly than her husband, Lillian recognizes that the mill workers are not just cogs in a machine, that some are family men and that their children might grow up to be something other than lumbermen—indeed she responds to Randolph's suggestion otherwise, asking, "How much timber will be left when these children are old enough to cut it? . . . Times are changing up ahead," she points out to him (162). Lillian has come a long way from the woman who "could not function living alone" (104–5), the change having begun in

New Orleans where, rather than being "lonely and homesick," as Randolph feared she would be, "she seemed delighted to be out on her own" and where she developed pride in her husband's efforts to help his brother and "no longer complained that Randolph was dull" (131). When he visited her in New Orleans, Randolph had found her residence there "wastefully comfortable, so bright it hurt his eyes with its white plaster medallions and ivory walls" (130), but Lillian adapts quickly to her quite different surroundings when she moves from New Orleans to Nimbus: "She learned the necessity of keeping a shovel on the front porch, which she used to cut the heads off snakes sunning on the steps in the afternoons" (161). Still, she asserts that one can build a community in a swamp: "Every mill town has a school and church, Rand. It's time you think about providing some civilization" (163).

Gautreaux follows this conversation with a brief section describing the first church service, the attendance at which surprised Randolph: "To his amazement, he counted many heads, and as he walked up he saw that the rough benches were filled with women, and their men were standing along the walls. Outside, Negro workers and their women gathered under the windows to hear the spilled-over preaching." Even the men without women hang out in the periphery: "A gang of young bucks was sitting in the commissary yard on upright bolts of cypress. . . . Three white sawyers sat behind them on the commissary porch, quietly chewing and whittling, their ears turned toward the overflowing schoolhouse. The boiler gang lounged about the double doors to the steam plant, far out of earshot, but watching, nevertheless." Lillian, Randolph realizes, was right: "Scanning the yard again he understood that the school and church had become in one day the hub of the rude wheel that was Nimbus" (164). Further confirming Lillian's recognition of the value of churches and schools, juxtaposed against this scene is a brief section back in the community called Tiger Island (the name of the town in *The Next Step in the Dance*), where Father Schultz is distraught over a young local who has become one of Buzetti's prostitutes, reminding the reader that buildings alone do not provide civilization.

Ironically, when Randolph and Lillian return to Pennsylvania for Christmas, they find themselves "no longer fond of snow and bland food" and, after their visit, gladly "traveled back South to . . . Nimbus, that place tethered to all of civilization only by a few miles of buckled railroad," that place where they understand the value of such dichotomies as "ignorance and good food, poverty and independence" (168). As Adam and Eve learned in the garden, one can only appreciate good by knowing evil. And in spite of all its progress, Nimbus remains a violent place. Many men still frequent the saloon, and one night it is Randolph who must shoot one man to save another.

In spite of her development since moving to Louisiana, Lillian responds to the news of Randolph's violent act in the same way that Randolph earlier responded to Byron's—with implicit accusation and judgment: "You came here to straighten Byron out. Instead you're doing the same" (179). Even after finally offering him comfort when he wakes up crying in the night, "cradling his head against her breasts and telling him it was all right what he had done, that she could forgive him," she still responds to his asking her, "How else could I have handled it?" very much as he answered Byron earlier, "Let the other men die, I guess," although by this time in their lives, Gautreaux interjects, "they both knew [this] was no answer at all" (183).

Just knowing they no longer have all the answers is progress for Randolph and Lillian, and both are slowly growing up as they understand more and more of the fallen world. One issue that they do not take far into consideration as they try to build a better civilization for the descendants of the mill workers is race relations. As noted in the passages quoted previously, the church is segregated: the black families are listening to the preaching from outside the church doors until they have their own church. Lillian does offer places for schooling the black children and where the black church services can be held, but when Randolph had broached the subject of adopting Walter just after May's death, Lillian rejected the idea in favor of just taking the child in as a ward. She claimed concern for Walter (how he would feel upon discovering he had been lied to should the truth of his parentage later emerge), but most likely she was really concerned about her own social position if his racial makeup were discovered, since she and Randolph are planning to return to their former lives once this swamp is cleared. There is no reason that Walter's identity would be revealed, for though Lillian suggests that the revelation might come about through visits from Byron and Ella, the reader knows this couple has no plans to return to Pittsburgh. In fact, Ella says as much as she makes her peace with mothering another woman's child (during which Walter's mixed race is not a factor): "It sure would be hard to let you off the hook if we were in one of our hometowns. . . . But here, well, where the hell are we, anyway?" (286). And at the end of the novel, as the brothers break down the mill now that all of the trees are cleared, the lumber shipped out, we learn that Byron and Ella are off to Oregon. He will join the family business after all, but in the West, far from anyone who knows Walter's true identify (including Randolph).

The reader presumes that Randolph and Lillian will return to Pittsburgh, that Randolph will assume his now very much *earned* place as CEO of the business (in contrast to Byron's destined place as first born). But the younger couple is on a productive track of their own, Lillian encouraging family-centered communities with the schools built of the Aldridges' lumber. Gautreaux provides no fairy tale ending, but as he says, "There is still light in this novel. It's not a pessimistic book. It doesn't have an unhappy ending. There are many negative developments in it, but there are positive evolutions too" (Fitten, 104). One might consider, for example, Byron's answer to Randolph's "How are you" after they watch the "Last Tree" fall: "No better . . . but gladder to be here" (299), the positive qualification new since Lillian had asked Byron how he was when she first arrived and he answered simply, "More or less the same" (119). The addition to his earlier response also echoes Byron's response to Lillian's accusation that Randolph "seems sorry . . . but not all that sorry" after he had killed the man. "That's a good thing, to be glad to be alive" (233), Byron had told her, alluding to his own lack of appreciation of life prior to becoming Walter's father.

In contrast to his brother's earlier negative attitude toward life, as Randolph feared his own impending death after being shot, he had felt a "great pain welling up inside him [that] had nothing to do with a bullet" (277) but rather was sorrow over leaving his life and the woman and brother he loves. And at novel's end, with his new appreciation of the blessings in his life (even if they do not include being a father), he responds to Byron's concern about the blind horse left behind, the only thing from the mill they could not sell or even give away, "I'm not sure it's miserable. . . . It's just blind" (303). Like the horse, Randolph accepts his handicaps and is learning to get around with his new knowledge of the world, the understanding he perceives in the blind horse: "The animal had listened to everything coming apart and knew what was happening, that the human world was a temporary thing, a piece of junk that used up the earth and then was consumed itself by the world it tried to destroy. When Randolph understood what the animal knew, a bottomless sadness crawled over him like a winter fog come out of the swamp at night. He thought of the cottages and shutters made out of this woods and of the money in his Pennsylvania bank account, but looking at the horse he could see no worth in any of it." And yet he does not agree with Byron that it would be merciful to put the horse "out of its misery" (303), does not agree that the animal *is* so unhappy. He has realized the concept of the *felix culpa*—that there is a kind of satisfaction in knowledge, even if it is a depressing knowledge of the world. It is only in knowing evil that one understands good.[14]

Significantly, when the horse tries to follow the sound of their departure, Byron cranks up his Victrola, which is among the few traces of civilization left behind, and puts on one of the records that he sought comfort from during the darker days of his depression. This music, which served as Byron's link to his past before his brother came, whose meaning to Byron Randolph sought to discover in his efforts to help his brother, keeps the horse from following the two men. It remains, with plenty of grass to eat, in the clearing that Byron says "looks like France when I left it" (304) as the brothers leave for parts north and west, respectively, one back to civilization, the other to continue to civilize, both now aware of the consequences of uncivilized behavior but also understanding the redemptive power of love.

Gautreaux believes the reason "readers found some echoes of Conrad" in *The Clearing* is because "*The Clearing* deals with a man's separation from civilization and with the results of the separation." His explanation reflects again the value he places in "the moral role of fiction": "If a story or novel doesn't touch on a question of right and wrong, of good and evil, of indolence or personal striving . . . it isn't a complete tale." Once again, though, the dichotomy is not simplified in the novel. Gautreaux's realism is reflected in his understanding of life's contradictions: "As for Byron and Randolph finding clear answers of right and wrong, . . . life is not science and certainly religion is not science. The brothers understand that it is wrong to kill people. They also understand that morally they are allowed to preserve their lives and the lives of others, even if they have to kill someone in the process. Living with such contradictory notions gives them cosmic pain and keeps them thinking at all times about the consequences of their actions."[15] Gautreaux contrasts his own work with a common "type of story I run across . . . a truly dark narrative about vicious people who don't learn anything from what they do and are not punished in any way and never get their comeuppance." While he recognizes that "sometimes that's realism," he also believes that "it's unrealistic to ignore compassion and the ability people have to cope and even triumph over their problems" (Bauer, "Interview"). In Gautreaux's fiction, even this darker novel and his next, which includes similar violent elements not commonly found in his short stories or the first novel, the villains usually "get their comeuppance," while the protagonists are rewarded for learning from their mistakes, and the reader closes Gautreaux's books more satisfied by the justice implicit in their happy endings.

The Missing

A boy who'd grown up in Sam's hometown had died en route of a burst appendix and was buried at sea after a perfunctory prayer. Sam and several other Louisiana men had stood in snow flurries on the fantail and watched the shrouded figure bob in the ship's rolling wake, refusing to sink, as though the corpse itself didn't feel right about the lead-cold sea and was trying to drift back toward the warm soil of a Louisiana graveyard. He was a Duplechen boy, his father a wiry little farmer who was good with mules. Sam knew the man and could imagine his sorrow, the vacant place at his table, the forever-broken link.

Gautreaux returns to the post–World War I era in his next novel, *The Missing*, in which music plays a major role again as well, for much of the novel is set aboard an entertainment steamboat traveling up and down the Mississippi. The protagonist of this novel, Sam Simoneaux, is a Cajun, in contrast to the Aldridge brothers of *The Clearing*, but like Colette Thibodeaux of the first novel, he is seeking to rise above his raising, a goal that keeps him from dealing with his troubling family history until almost the end of the novel and thus from figuring out what is at the heart of his failures—to both himself and others.

The Missing opens with a ship of American soldiers heading to France, who are surprised to find dancing in the streets upon their arrival—it is November 11, 1918, Armistice Day: "Many cheered, but a portion of the young recruits seemed disappointed that they wouldn't get to shoot at anybody. . . . Sam wondered what he would tell his friends back home of his war experience. The most valuable trophies of war were stories, and this one was good only for a derisive laugh" (4). As in *The Clearing*, with this third novel Gautreaux continues his deconstruction of romantic notions of war and his exploration of the ravages of war that persist after peace is declared. Gautreaux notes that the two novels are comparable "because in one, we have a protagonist severely damaged by his experience in World War I, and in the second we have a protagonist who arrives in France on the day the armistice is signed and doesn't get to shoot anybody at all," although with this lack of experience the new novel's protagonist is reminiscent of Randolph Aldridge, who did not experience the war that scarred his brother.[1]

Even without experiencing combat, it is not long before twenty-three-year-old Sam glimpses the reality of war when he is assigned to help clean up the mess left behind—"enough un-exploded grenades of all nationalities to keep him busy for a hundred years," for example. As Sam's company hikes through the ravaged landscape to explode as many of these as they can, "the smell was a walking presence and a mockery of what [Sam] had imagined of war, now blasted out of his mind forever. He understood how brutally the illusion of warfare had ended for the hundreds of thousands who'd struggled here. 'What a damned lie,' he said aloud" (9). Sam also witnesses the physical pain of a soldier hurt during this cleanup and "sensed how minuscule this pain was compared to the vast agonies of the death field they were in" (11). And then he becomes participatory in causing some of this pain when his company inadvertently blasts the home of an already orphaned girl when they overshoot their target trying to blow up an ammunition depot.

Disgusted with himself for their carelessness, Sam tries to help the wounded child but then must abandon her, and the memory of her will haunt him until the very end of the novel.

Significantly Gautreaux inserts the story of Sam's own tragic past into the novel just before Sam's encounter with the French girl. The reader realizes that this orphaned child mirrors Sam's own past, although Sam has no memory of his parents and siblings, who were all brutally murdered when he was still a baby. As Sam cleans his boots of mud that is likely "composed of atomized blood and shell-fractured bone," he is reminded "of how the dead men's families were maimed by the loss that for some would surely grow larger over time, the absence more palpable than the presence" (13), which he knows from the experience of his own loss of a child, who died of a fever, and which he will eventually realize about this own lost though unremembered parents. Sam's recognition of the dead as not just "heroes but also pieces cut forever out of the lives of their families" makes him long to see the uncle who raised him and then who "moved one chair out to the back porch when Sam had left the farm so they could remember him by its absence" (14).

That is the only way that Sam can remember his parents—by their absence. His uncle Claude has told him very little beyond the basics of what happened to them, not wanting to spoil the innocence he believes every child deserves by going into the details of the killings. The outline of the story is horrible enough: Sam's father accidentally killed a man who was torturing a horse, and members of the man's family came to Sam's home one day and sprayed gunfire through the walls of their house. When the murderers went inside to kill anyone not yet dead, they did not find the six-month-old baby (Sam), who had been thrown into the stove by his dying father for protection against the flying bullets and the madmen behind the guns. When Claude arrived to find his brother's family butchered, he hears the baby, crying with hunger but then smiling when his uncle opened the stove, oblivious to the horror Claude is observing around them. Claude is determined that his nephew might remain oblivious and so does not share the details with Sam, merely telling his young charge that the worst horror is in the souls of those who would commit such a crime. Thus does Sam not grow up with the kind of vigilante mentality that drove these unknown killers to avenge their kinsman's accidental death on an innocent woman and her children, as well as the man they blame for their loss.

In contrast to Sam, the wounded French girl he finds outside the house looks at him with "watery and old" eyes (23). Her childhood innocence has certainly been cut short. Wise beyond her years, the child aptly identifies Sam as she says he should be called *Chanceux*, knowing only what he tells her about arriving on the day of the Armistice, while Sam recognizes what an appropriate name this is for the baby who survived when his whole family was killed. Accepting his *bonne chance*, in contrast to all he has witnessed of the war he missed, as well as what he has been told about his own past, Sam takes the nickname home with him, introducing himself as Lucky to those he meets. Even his wife picks up the new moniker.

Sam's luck seems to continue upon his return to Louisiana. He and his wife move to New Orleans, where he works on "getting rid of his bayou accent" and finds a job as a floorwalker in a department store (29). He enjoys his job, happy to be out of the hot sun of farmwork, but his luck seems to run out one day when parents lose their child in the store and his failure to follow the store's procedures for how to respond when a child is separated from parents results in the little girl's abduction. Once again Sam feels responsible for the lost innocence of a child due in part to his own carelessness, and in this novel, the reader realizes, Gautreaux continues his development of his recurring conflict regarding taking responsibility, regardless of the extent of one's blame. Certainly it is not Sam's fault that an unscrupulous man decided that this talented daughter of a show couple would be an ideal present for his wife, who wants a child but can't seem to have one and finds the children she meets at orphanages too needy. But Sam accepts blame for the missing child and generously does not point out in his own defense the parents' failure to keep an eye on their daughter.

One is reminded that Sam's uncle did not teach his orphaned nephew to hold a grudge when, though he is fired after the kidnapping, Sam agrees to try to help Ted and Elise Weller find their daughter. Of course he is now unemployed, with medical bills to pay (he was knocked out by one of the kidnappers just as he came upon the missing child in a dressing room, drugged and shorn of her curls), so the girl's parents get him a job on the showboat they work on, and the department store owner does say that if Sam finds the girl he will consider reemployment. But, already haunted by one girl whose suffering he was a party to causing, Sam wishes to dispel this second haunting face from his dreams. And as a man who had his whole family taken from him and who lost a child himself, Sam is sympathetic to the Wellers' sudden loss of their daughter. He agrees to crew on the steamboat as it travels up and down the Mississippi in order to watch the audiences for the face of the woman he saw briefly as she changed the drugged girl into the clothes of a little boy.

Chapter 6 provides the first interlude from the novel's main perspective (Sam's) to the Kentucky home of Acy White, a wealthy banker, and his wife, Willa, a forty-year-old heiress.

Unscrupulous Acy and sociopathic Willa are a good match for each other, but their voraciously sexual marriage has produced no children. As though buying her an expensive piece of jewelry, Acy has arranged the kidnapping of the talented three-year-old girl they saw on stage one night aboard an excursion steamboat. When we meet the Whites, young Lily Weller, now called Madeline, is calmly trying to figure out her new world order. She has been told her parents are dead and to call this new couple Mother and Daddy but *not* to call the "hillbilly" servant girl *Miss* Vessy, the latter instructions almost as disconcerting as new parents to a child who had thus far grown up among show people and sailors. Lily is not as "lucky" as Sam: when he lost his parents, he was still raised by people who shared his original family's values. In this chapter we also learn that the reason the Whites had not legitimately adopted some orphan is that, ironically, Willa found such children too *un*lucky and decided "she wanted . . . a child fortunate enough to be currently loved" (58). A woman whose lack of scruples puts her on a par with the "hillbillies" (as she might call them) who took Sam's family from him, Willa felt no qualms about taking away another mother's child, perhaps because of her own inability to love. Our first glimpse, then, of the couple who has "adopted" Lily bodes ill for the little girl, even if she is dressed up now in the finest clothes and seems to be physically unharmed and unthreatened.

Back on board the steamboat, Sam is discovering that with a little alcohol many otherwise law-abiding citizens become violent and unruly, and his duties are not just those of a third mate but also a bouncer's. The novel's setting calls to mind Mark Twain's riverboat stories until Sam recognizes the female kidnapper and traces her back into the swamp, where scene and events become more darkly Faulknerian than humorously Twainian.

But once again Gautreaux's hero is no son of the aristocracy out of place in the swamp like Faulkner's Gowan Stephens and Horace Benbow finding themselves among the bootleggers in *Sanctuary*. Purposely unarmed (knowing he will be no match for them), Sam confronts the kidnappers, Ninga Skadlock and her sons, and they let him leave unharmed.

Interestingly, while Ninga does not admit to kidnapping the child, her remarks about the grieving parents are another example in the novel in which seemingly very different people ultimately have more in common than they would guess. Ninga rejects Sam's attempt to get her to commiserate with the worried parents, suggesting that the child might be better off in different circumstances. She tells Sam that "sometimes people seem one way on the surface. But inside, they're different. . . . Those fine parents might be musicians, all right, the drifter kind that think they're better than everybody else just because they can read squiggles on a set of lines. . . . Rummies in the vaudeville orchestra, whorehouse bands, saloon singers." And, to Sam's objection and assurance that the Wellers "aren't like that," she asks, "Still, where will they be in ten years?" (84). Ninga, it turns out, is right: people can be very different from how they appear, for Sam, who has thus far acted sympathetically and unselfishly in this novel, surprises the reader when he finds the girl at the Whites' residence but, attracted by Lily's new surroundings, tells no one of her whereabouts. His reaction to what the Whites can provide in contrast to what life as a Weller offers is the same as Ninga Skadlock had suggested. Considering how Sam has rejected his own farm upbringing, even the language of his French heritage, the reader should not, after all, be so surprised that he would have his head turned by the pretty dress he sees on the child and the big yard he finds her playing in. This man who has not attempted to find out more about his own parents even now that he is no longer a child to be protected against such dark knowledge—indeed, has witnessed the horrors of war and suffered the loss of his own child—allows himself to believe that a child might be better off with people so unscrupulous as to take her away from her parents than with the mother who loves her but, widowed by this time, has very little to offer, in Sam's view.

But before Sam is distracted by the Whites' wealth in his search for Lily, the novel is very reminiscent of Mark Twain's work; the different people Sam meets up and down the Mississippi call to mind the various characters in *Adventures of Huckleberry Finn*. One lead sends Sam to a farmer who has recently taken in a mysterious child—a boy, it turns out—rescuing him from the abusive man who had adopted him for hard labor and sexual abuse. This farmer echoes the mindset of Sam's uncle Claude (as well as the story "Resistance" in *Welding with Children*) as he explains to Sam the reason for his intercession on the child's behalf: "We never forget those five years or so when we're kids. When we're looked after. . . . Not hurt by our elders unless we do somethin' to deserve it. . . . When we're little shavers we don't think there's nothin' bad in the world, and nothin' that can make us hurt. If we do get a little pain we kin put our face on our daddy's shirt or momma's dress and it'll go away" (133–34), which this man hopes is what he'll find heaven to be like. At the end of this conversation the farmer, the son of a lawman, gives Sam the family name of the people who may have been Sam's family's murderers: the Cloats, a clan so corrupted by their anger and violence, Sam will eventually learn, that their children never do get that age of innocence that his uncle and this kind stranger preserve for orphaned boys.

Ironically the consequences of Sam's role in the kidnapping of the missing girl extend to abbreviating her brother August's period of childhood innocence. When Sam returns from this mistaken lead, he finds August ecstatic over the opportunity the steamboat captain has offered him to perform that night: "The boy's feet were dancing when Sam waved him off, watching him run, trying to remember the last time he'd felt that excitement boiling in his own feet, so happy at fitting in and doing well that the future seemed to promise just one long, ecstatic performance" (136). But unbeknown to August, his father, having found his way to the Skadlocks' place after being unsatisfied by the lack of immediate results from Sam's visit with them, has been mangled by their dog. Ted Weller is by this time lying in a hospital with injuries he will ultimately die from, so August's euphoria is short lived; it is not long before he is grieving with his widowed mother over a second empty place at their table.

Even as the novel makes its case for forgiveness rather than reprisal, the author, with his usual ability to examine issues from both sides, explores the desire for vengeance. Sam's shipboard bunkmate Charlie Duggs harshly criticizes Sam's failure to seek out his family's killers. As Byron Aldridge and the marshal try to tell Randolph in *The Clearing*, Charlie notes that if you "kill a snake, . . . the next man on the trail won't get bit" (160). Charlie's goading is part of what motivates Sam to ask questions about his own family's killers as the steamboat approaches Arkansas, where the killers are purported to have come from. Charlie's bravado may not be what this novel ultimately condones, but his needling evokes the realization that Sam has really not yet understood what his uncle was trying to teach him about there being no need to avenge their family members' deaths: Claude believes the killers are punished enough by being who they are. But at this point in the novel, Sam tells Charlie, "My uncle never raised me to be big on revenge. . . . Most French people on the bayou are like that. *Too poor to afford a grudge*" (159; emphasis added). Lack of blood money is definitely not at the heart of Uncle Claude's peaceful heart. Indeed the killers who were avenging their kinsman were even poorer than Sam's family. Once again, then, Sam's failure to act is connected to his materialism, which is what allows him to look past the Whites' behavior to their wealth and decide not to tell Lily's family when he finds her.

Soon after Ted Weller's death, Sam finds out his own wife is expecting a baby, and shortly after that, he finds Lily but fails to report her whereabouts to her grieving mother and brother. It is not until his own child is born, and Sam "couldn't imagine being without him," understanding that "if anyone took him away, it would be like losing a part of himself" (192), that he realizes his mistake. With the birth of this second son, he misses his first son even more, regrets the lost family members whose features he cannot recognize in his newborn's face, and understands the magnitude of what he has done to Elsie Weller in keeping from her the whereabouts of her child. He also realizes how difficult it will be to undo what he has done, for he will have to admit to a child's mother that he had decided another woman would be a better parent. Elsie's fury with Sam is understandable, and to make matters worse, by the time Sam goes after the child, the Skadlock sons (whose mother has died by this time) have decided to kidnap Lily again in order to get more money out of the Whites.

The reader will notice at the point of the story when Sam recognizes his mistake in keeping Lily's location secret and it feels like the central problem (the missing child) is on its way to a resolution that the novel is only half over. It does take several more suspenseful chapters before Lily is reunited with her mother and brother, but even then the novel has a ways to go, for this central plot element is still only what leads Sam to recognize his own loss and its consequences to his seemingly lucky life. Earlier in the novel, observing August Weller before his father's death, Sam had "tried to remember himself at fourteen, when some days he knew for sure that everything was going to turn out well, that nothing else bad could possibly happen to anyone he was close to, that life would treat him fairly. He'd felt this way up until his first son died. And then there were the sorrows of France, where he finally understood that the family stories weren't legends, but reports of real killings" (100–101). In spite of the death of his firstborn, ever since the horrors he witnessed in France, he has called himself Lucky as though the nickname could serve as a charm to protect his loved ones. But now Sam is wondering how lucky anyone could be whose whole family was murdered, even if he did survive. Sam is only just beginning to feel the "empty chair blues" (which Gautreaux had at one point titled this novel) that he has previously recognized others around him suffering. What follows the return of Lily to her mother and brother is as compelling as her second kidnapping and rescue.

As Ralph Skadlock kidnaps Lily from the Whites, Gautreaux again turns a villain into a human being deserving of sympathy for his own brutal childhood, which led him on the path to the criminal life he has taken. As Vessy helps Ralph to sneak the child away, she, too, is characterized as more than just a hillbilly, the label her employers have given her, thus blinding themselves to her shrewdness and ingenuity. Even Acy White is given a humanizing scene, when he misses the child's voice and wonders briefly if this is how her parents had felt. To rescue Lily, Sam must speak French to a mule (thus does Gautreaux humorously make Sam return to the Cajun heritage he has been denying), and he has the chance to save August from the fate of his father and to teach August the lesson about revenge that Uncle Claude taught Sam.

Sam is on his way to redemption for the misplaced values that led him to delay this family's reunion. After finally touching the child he has been looking for since the novel's beginning, Sam dreams of being "in someone's lap, a man, judging from the smell of kerosene and wood smoke and a little gale of beer breathed over his head; his stomach felt full, and a callused hand pressed down on it as though holding a jewel secure" (285). Whereas previously Sam seems to have felt that he couldn't mourn what he never knew, recently he has envied August's memories of his father, even as he recognizes that such memories have caused a more immediate sense of loss than Sam has ever felt. This flash of memory, then, is a bittersweet gift to the man who is finally acknowledging the loss of his parents.

Sam is *not*, however, rewarded with his old job back, so he returns to the steamboat, where he witnesses how the relatively short time Lily was missing (less than a year) has been enough to affect her personality. She is no longer satisfied with a rag doll, when she had numerous dolls at the Whites' house, and the child who could not understand the Whites' perception of the difference between herself and Vessy makes an unconsciously but no less insensitive racist remark to one of the steamboat's wait staff. Without her father, who Sam recognizes had the real "musical spark" in the family, "Lily would still sing, but she might never again perform" (294). And the bitterness of her mother, which Sam endures patiently, is also bound to have an effect on the little girl, as it does on Sam, who no longer thinks of himself as lucky: "He knew [now] that event followed event, and that it was his bad luck to be first in a string of bad fortune" (299).

Rather than lash out at Elsie Weller (he again rejects the idea of asking her "what she and Ted were doing the moment the child was spirited away from them" [299]), Sam continues in his endeavors to make up for his own past mistakes, including his failure to show any interest in the family he lost and his neglect of the one who took him in. In order to better understand what August and Lily are missing, Sam goes to see his uncle to learn more about his own father and mother. Sam begins with the subject of his parents' killers, but Claude emphasizes the impossibility of revenge, saying, "You can kill 'em dead with a axe and they won't even understand why you doin' it." Claude reminds Sam of the lesson he has tried to convey since first telling him about the killing of his family: "What people do wrong is its own punishment. . . . I rather be your dead papa for five minutes than one of them killers for a whole life" (308). Claude then gives Sam another gift of memory, telling him about Sam's father's fiddle playing, and "a new door opened in Sam's head, and through it came notes and rhythm flowing onto a cypress porch" (309). Sam leaves with his father's fiddle and a reconnection to and renewed appreciation of his uncle, aunt, and cousins.

When Sam returns, he finds that the flu has infected the steamboat performers and crew, including Elsie Weller, who gives her children over to his protection before she dies—even as she still insists, "It's all your fault" (318). Her message seems to be that he must take care of them because he is responsible for their being orphans. Giving him her children does not mean she forgives him, but the reader understands by this time that Sam does not need forgiveness, he needs to forgive, as implied by his uncle, who asked him when he persisted in the subject of finding his family's killers, "You gonna find 'em to forgive 'em?" (309). Witnessing four-year-old Lily's uncomprehending sadness over the loss of her mother, Sam "felt sick for her, but terrible for himself as well, for the thin shoulder he cupped in his right hand might have been his own sister's or brother's, and then he was crushed by a deeper understanding of what he had lost back before he knew what loss was. He didn't know such a feeling could come so late, and to keep from crying in front of her, he grabbed a music book and started playing the first piece that opened up" (325). Ted is not there to teach his daughter music; Sam's father was not there to teach him. But now the older orphan will teach the younger, and perhaps they will both have some semblance of what they would otherwise miss.

Sam brings the children home to his wife but must then return to the steamboat to work, for now there are more mouths to feed. Upon Sam's arrival, the pilot praises him for taking in the children, and when Sam remarks upon his sense of responsibility to them, the pilot responds (expressing a typical Gautreaux theme), "We're all responsible for something, but most of us don't do a damn thing about it" (332). Sam has also apparently determined that it is his responsibility to seek out his family's killers, though for what reason he still does not know. Once again he finds answers as he travels up the Mississippi toward Arkansas, where he meets a Constable Soner, who has had his own tragic encounter with the Cloats, the likely killers of Sam's family. Soner invites Sam into his barricaded home; listens to Sam's family history; and, to discourage the younger man from pursuing the amoral and violent killers, shares his own history with the Cloats, which has left him alone, afraid, and maimed—though like Claude, Soner spares Sam the worst of the details.

Echoing Claude as well, Soner tries to tell Sam that it is the Cloats who are worse off, even compared to their victims and their victims' survivors: "The Cloats go through life incurious about anything at all, whether history or music or the well-being of their own blood," which Soner contrasts with Sam's "quest for knowledge" upon hearing from Sam that he is not seeking them out to kill them. Just as Gautreaux touched upon themes in *The Clearing* that go back to the story of Adam and Eve in the garden, here too he alludes to this earliest of stories as he distinguishes Sam from the Cloats, who are "like animals, interested only in what's in front of them at the moment," and to the concept of the *fortunate* fall: Sam is "lucky," the constable says, for being curious (341). He is a flawed (fallen) human being, but he is not so depraved as the Cloats, whom Soner also distinguishes from animals by their one ambition—not the fruit of knowledge but "revenge" (342). Soner understands, as the marshal recognized about the villains in *The Clearing*, that the Cloats are "exactly like you and I. They've just fallen a few more rungs down the moral ladder than most" (346).

Still Sam must see for himself that he is, after all, lucky—lucky not to be a Cloat. No longer trusting this perception of his good fortune, he is not sure that the only real revenge is simply not being a Cloat. "They live in their chosen isolation so that nothing good can touch them. And they insist on seeing themselves as normal, abetting each other's notions," Soner tells him, so revenge from their victims' survivors would only confirm their worldview. Most of them, it has turned out, have died off, ultimately victims of their own decadence. By the time Sam reaches the surviving Cloats, whom he finds living (or rather, dying) in the most disgusting of conditions, he understands how right Soner was that "the worst thing that ever happened to them is each other" (346).

So what does Sam gain from this visit? The man who had remarked to Charlie Duggs upon the absence of even any pictures of his family is rewarded for his efforts to find his family's killers—and not in order to kill them—with just that: pictures of his family, as well as the satisfaction he might be able to feel in having one of these depraved human beings admit to having *seen*, really seen, the people they killed:

> "The woman was on her stomach and the girl was under her left arm."
>
> "What color was their hair?"
>
> "Damn it to hell, I can't recollect that. Don't you know?"
>
> [Sam] got down on his knees and put the pistol on the edge of the blanket. "You've got to understand. That's why I'm here. I never saw my mamma's hair."
>
> . . . "It was brown. . . . Clean. And so was the little girl's." (355–56)

Once started, the murderer is also able to remember that Sam's brother "had him on a new bandanna," and he recalls that Sam's father "was startin' to bald. Ain't that picture enough for you?" Not quite done, Sam asks him where his father had fallen. "Dead agin the stove," the Cloat responds, and Gautreaux adds, showing perhaps that this depraved man has finally been moved by the horror of his actions, "His eyes blinked and watered with the pain of telling" (356). The dying man could just be in physical pain, but his apparent terror of the hog rooting outside suggests that in spite of his adamant insistence that there is no hell after death, he is afraid for himself; his actions trouble him after all, now that he faces his impending death.

Sam leaves, knowing for certain now that his uncle has been right about the Cloats and with "details . . . about his family [that might] sprout memories he never had, or would've had" (358), which seems to be what Sam had been missing and needing all along. He shares this gift with Soner, who takes the boards off his windows and lets Sam play his long untouched piano as they celebrate their inability to understand people like the Cloats. Their merrymaking, according to the narrator, might have led "a murderer crouching in the wind-rattled weeds [to be] distracted from his plans, envious of the good time" (359). On his way back to his family, then, Sam happens upon a piano, left out in the rain during shipment to its new owner, who therefore refused delivery, another stroke of good fortune for Lucky Sam, who is not so particular, knowing the value is in the musician more so than the instrument.

There is one more step in Sam's conflict resolution. He has searched for and found the missing child and in doing so realized the loss of his own family—and with that recognition he has reconnected with the heritage he thought he could so easily dismiss. Upon his return from gathering pictures from which he might make memories, not only does he have a new piano, on which he can at least try to teach Lily what her absent father would have taught her, but also it is not long before he receives a letter from the French girl whose house his company had destroyed. The novel "com[es] full circle," first with this return to the issue of war, its lasting destruction, and the importance of some kind of humanity in the midst of all that violence. The woman (who was that child) writes, "When I think of that final blast, I marvel that it was followed by a messenger who tried to comfort me . . . that is the way it ought to be. If each artillery shell had an escort, each bullet, each aerial bomb was followed by a soldier who would arrive and look around and ask 'Is everyone all right? How can I help?' then war would not last so long or be so bad." This is similar to what Sam learned about what drove the Cloats' violence and thus led to their degeneracy and destruction. At the root of their revenge was simply malevolence, and Claude knew that their corruption could happen to any man who forgot that his victims were human beings. Going after even the Cloats or dropping bombs on people one never sees turns humans into unthinking murderers. Claude's lesson had apparently influenced Sam's character long before he really understood it, for he went to find out if anyone was hurt by the explosion that happened when he was in charge. He recognized that there might be someone upon whom the ammunition for which he was responsible fell. And thus, as the French woman tells him, he gave her "nine reasons for gratitude"—the nine fingers she had left after the blast, which she believes were saved because he stopped to help her: "If you had not blown apart my house I might have starved or lost heart. I've learned to take the good with the bad and want to thank you again, not for the explosion, but for your wonderful visit" (366).

With this release of the guilt that has haunted him since the war, Sam is ready to help Lily (now eight) and thus is another circle completed. He brings this orphan to the home that took him in, as well as to the home of Sam's parents, where Sam is able to pass on Claude's lesson to Lily. When Lily complains about the injustice in the fact that the people who killed Sam's family "lived out their lives" (372), Sam asks her, "People who would do this. What kind of life do you think they had?" (373). In contrast to what we saw of the surviving Cloats, whose house is already falling down around them before their deaths, Sam's first home is in a state of destruction because of the bullet holes and resulting absence of anyone living there. And reminding Sam of the more important difference between the two domains, in the middle of this crumbling house stands a big stove in which a man hid his baby, thus ensuring that his bloodline, people capable of love and not driven by senseless vengeance, would continue for many more generations.

Sam took this journey home to help Lily, and she helps him in return. While he rejects her suggestion to bring the stove home as a souvenir, he does allow her to bring home the washboard she finds. First he is concerned that it will "just keep me looking back" (374), but then Lily's response echoes that of the French woman: "It doesn't have to make you think only about the bad things." Although he can't "remember any good things," she reminds him that the washboard could be a catalyst for "'imagin[ing] what happened before those.' She pointed to the bullet holes" (375); that is, his mother's washboard would remind him of the prelapsarian world of the baby who knew love, rather than vengeance.

Once again in this ending the reader finds the optimistic vision that distinguishes Gautreaux's work from that of many of his predecessors and contemporaries. One might, for example, contrast Sam and his successful rescue of Lily with, as mentioned previously, Faulkner's Horace Benbow, whose rescue of Temple Drake from her kidnapper was not so successful in *Sanctuary*. While the reader perceives hope for Lily, Temple seems irreparably damaged by her experience. And the Weller children's ultimate acceptance of Sam and his wife as their surrogate parents is also quite different from the ending of another novel mentioned before, *Joe*, by Gautreaux's contemporary Larry Brown, in which Gary rejects Joe's offer of a permanent home, choosing to return to take care of his mother and sister and leaving Joe to avenge the violent molestation of Gary's young sister, which will inevitably send Joe back to jail. Brown's novel comes to a close with a final violent act, contrasting significantly with the quiet departure of Gautreaux's Sam and Lily, heading home to his wife and her new mother and leaving this violent interlude in their lives behind, the reader feels certain, forever.

Afterword

> I've learned that every little neighborhood contains all the
> universal themes any writer needs.

In 1979, after noting the absence of an authentic Cajun voice in
literature, folklorist Dave Peyton remarked that he had "no
doubt there will be Cajun literature in the future. The area is too
fertile and alive with stories, traditions, and legends to remain
fallow forever." Peyton also noted in this interview that "the
[Cajun] tradition [was] completely oral but the body of stories,
songs and tales is very large,"[1] so it should not be surprising that
one of the Cajun writers who began to record a written body of
literature is a master storyteller as well as a talented musician.
Tim Gautreaux's contribution to southern letters is an insider's
view of Cajun culture more authentic than previous depictions
of Cajuns in fiction and film. He also adds to the blue-collar
voices provided by other contemporary southern writers, voices
previously confined to the margins of earlier generations' writ-
ings and often caricatured by them. And finally his heroes are
men of action intent upon bringing change to the contemporary
South rather than the Hamlet-like worriers of earlier southern
literature, who merely lament the lack of change in the post–
Civil War South.

As I noted in my 2005 book *William Faulkner's Legacy*,
which includes a chapter contrasting Gautreaux's blue-collar
white male protagonists with the white male descendants of the

Old South aristocracy at the center of most of Faulkner's fiction, "I don't know if Tim Gautreaux was or is consciously frustrated with the impotence of Faulkner's gentry (or with Faulkner's depiction of poor whites and 'white trash' in his fiction). I do know that for every two men who stumble upon a 'victim' in Gautreaux's fiction, one of them *does something* about the situation. Thus, while Gautreaux does not romanticize all Cajun 'day laborers' [as Faulkner has referred to blue-collar workers] into knights in shining armor, he does allow many of these blue-collar workers to do what they can to alleviate the suffering of others."[2] Such a character type is a significant change from previous depictions of the poor white man in literature, including the blue-collar characters of many of Gautreaux's own contemporaries. In his 2000 monograph *After Southern Modernism: Fiction of the Contemporary South*, Matthew Guin focuses on Dorothy Allison, Larry Brown, and Harry Crews in his exploration of this character type in contemporary southern fiction, observing how these three authors "opt for a realistic prose style that reflects the pessimism of their backgrounds."[3] Tim Gautreaux's much more positive view of his home region provides a refreshing perspective on the often criticized South. Unlike Faulkner's Quentin Compson, Tim Gautreaux does not have to convince himself that he does not "hate the South."

Mississippi writer Larry Brown praised Tim Gautreaux's *The Clearing*, saying, "This novel soars in its evocation of a land and people lost to the mists of times. It's a story of men and women bound to a great forest by their destruction of it, and the ties of family and blood and evil and greed and good and human tragedy and human triumph."[4] Hurricane Katrina brought tragic destruction to Gautreaux's (and my own) home state even as it occasioned stories of human triumph. The aftermath showed us all the ultimate fragility of civilization, and whatever is salvaged of the pre-Katrina New Orleans will be part of a new Louisiana, forever changed as the effects of the flood continue to ripple outward. What was Louisiana is, as Brown said of the period during which *The Clearing* is set, "lost to the mists of time"—except as it remains in memory, in history, in literature, reminding us of how important it is to have writers such as Tim Gautreaux.

Notes

Acknowledgments

1. L. Lamar Nisly, "A Catholic Who Happens to Write: An Interview with Tim Gautreaux," *Interdisciplinary Literary Studies* 8, no. 2 (2007): 99.

Chapter 1—Introduction

Epigraph from Tim Gautreaux, quoted in Christopher Scanlan, "Tim Gautreaux," *Creative Loafing Atlanta,* June 17, 2004, http://atlanta.creativeloafing.com/gyrobase/tim_gautreaux/Content?oid=15955 (accessed May 7, 2009); subsequent quotations from this interview will be cited parenthetically.

1. Marcia Gaudet, "The Image of the Cajun in Literature," *Journal of Popular Culture* 23, no. 1 (1989): 77; subsequent quotations from this essay will be cited parenthetically.

2. See also Leonard Deutsch's 1979 interview with folklorist Dave Peyton. Remarking upon the absence of Cajun literature by Cajuns, Peyton also traces depictions of Cajuns from Longfellow to Gaines. Deutsch, "Cajun Culture: An Interview," *MELUS* 6, no. 1 (1979): 87.

3. James H. Dormon, *The People Called Cajuns: An Introduction to an Ethnohistory* (Lafayette: Center for Louisiana Studies, 1983), 36.

4. Alluding to Marcia Gaudet's essay on Cajuns in literature in her interview, Maria Hebert-Leiter asked Gautreaux about outsiders' literary "misrepresentation[s]" of Cajuns, to which he responded, "It's really almost impossible to understand a culture unless you live in it." Hebert-Leiter, "An Interview with Tim Gautreaux," *Carolina Quarterly* 57, no. 2 (2005): 70; subsequent quotations from this interview will be cited parenthetically.

5. Christopher Joyal, "An Interview with Tim Gautreaux," *New Delta Review* 16, no. 1 (1998): 94.

6. Marc Fitten, "A Conversation with Tim Gautreaux," *Chattahoochee Review* 24, no. 1 (2003): 106–7.

7. Besides noting that every writer is regional, Gautreaux explains his resistance to the southern writer label as "a trick I play on myself. If people tell you you're a Southern writer and you believe it, you put yourself in a little claustrophobic room, you restrict the way you look at the world and when you go to write, you say to yourself, 'Let's see, I've got to have some alligators in here and some French accordion music and a sheriff with mirrored sunglasses.' In other words, you start thinking in clichés. You can't let yourself think like that or else you'll be, as Walker Percy once stated, in the business of amazing Yankees. So I'm not a Southern writer. I'm just a writer who lives in the South." Scanlan, "Tim Gautreaux."

8. In the same interview in which he noted the numerous other occupations of his time that have kept his writing output relatively modest, Gautreaux explained, "I write, but I don't look at myself as a writer. . . . I think it's almost important not to think of yourself in that one dimension. I do lots of things; writing is one of them. Ambition has never been my long suit, and that's one thing that marks me as a Louisiana native. It's nice that the appreciation of what I do as a writer happens. Yet if nobody published any of my stuff, I would still write." Christina Masciere, "Novel Approach: Tim Gautreaux Takes 'The Next Step,'" *New Orleans Magazine,* March 1998, 47; subsequent quotations from this interview will be cited parenthetically.

9. The writers who selected stories for the volumes of *The Best American Short Stories* in which Gautreaux's work has appeared include E. L. Doctorow, Garrison Keillor, Annie Proulx, Robert Stone, and Amy Tan.

10. *Kirkus Reviews,* September 11, 1996, 991.

11. Rand Richards Cooper, "Local Color," *Commonweal,* November 8, 1996, 25.

12. Perry Glasser, "True Dirt," *North American Review,* March–April 1997, 45.

13. Andy Solomon, Books in Brief: Fiction, *New York Times Book Review,* June 14, 1998, 21.

14. John Tait, review of *The Next Step in the Dance,* by Tim Gautreaux, *Missouri Review* 21, no. 2 (1998): 212.

15. Susan Larson, "The Writer Next Door," *New Orleans Times-Picayune,* March 15, 1998, E1.

16. Liam Callanan, "La. Stories," *New York Times Book Review,* October 3, 1999, 31.

17. Susan Balée, "Maximalist Fiction," *Hudson Review* 53, no. 3 (2000): 520, 519; emphasis added.

18. Alan Heathcock, Book Reviews, *Mid-American Review* 20 (2000): 249–50.

19. Bob Minzesheimer, "*Clearing* Is a Cut Above," *USA Today,* July 31, 2003, http://www.usatoday.com/life/books/reviews/2003-07-23-clearing_x.htm (accessed May 7, 2009).

20. The Critics: Briefly Noted, *New Yorker,* June 30, 2003, 101.

21. PW Forecasts: Fiction, *Publishers Weekly,* May 26, 2003, 49.

22. Alan Warner, "River of Blood," *Guardian* [UK], April 11, 2009, http://www.guardian.co.uk/books/2009/apr/11/the-missing-gautreaux-review (accessed April 28, 2009).

23. Doug Childers, "The Persistence of Memories." *Richmond Times-Dispatch,* April 28, 2009, http://www.timesdispatch.com/rtd/entertainment/books_literature/article/BMISS22_20090318-192903/235128/ (accessed April 28, 2009).

24. Jennifer Levasseur and Kevin Rabalais, "Interview with Tim Gautreaux," *Mississippi Review* 27, no. 3 (1999): 28; subsequent quotations from this interview will be cited parenthetically.

25. John Barth, "A Few Words About Minimalism," in *Further Fridays: Essays, Lectures, and Other Nonfiction, 1984–94,* by John Barth (Boston: Little, Brown, 1995), 65.

26. Matthew Guin, *After Southern Modernism: Fiction of the Contemporary South* (Jackson: University Press of Mississippi, 2000), xiii.

27. Pam Kingsbury, "'Everything Has a Purpose': An Interview with Tim Gautreaux," *Southern Scribe* 4, no. 8 (2003), http://www.southernscribe.com/zine/authors/Gautreaux_Tim.htm (accessed November 28, 2007).

Chapter 2—*Same Place, Same Things*

Epigraph from Tim Gautreaux quoted in Margaret D. Bauer, "An Interview with Tim Gautreaux: 'Cartographer of Louisiana Back Roads,'" *Southern Spaces,* May 28, 2009, http://www.southernspaces.org/contents/2009/bauer/1a.htm (accessed May 28, 2009); subsequent quotations from this interview will be cited parenthetically.

1. The point regarding Gautreaux's periodical publications is from a conversation I had with him at Longwood University, where I had the privilege of presenting the Dos Passos Prize to him on February 15, 2006.

2. Tim Gautreaux, *Same Place, Same Things* (New York: St. Martin's, 1996); quotations from this collection will be cited parenthetically.

3. Quoted from Elizabeth Arnold's interview with Gautreaux, "Best Short Stories 1997," *All Things Considered,* NPR, December 15, 1997. Gautreaux enumerates the "passes" he makes through a story in his *Atlantic Unbound* interview: "I . . . print out a first draft, and read for sentence structure. After edits I show it to someone (generally my wife or a graduate student I've worked with), and then I make five additional passes—each pass lasting about two and a half hours—before the manuscript is sent out for publication. On the first pass, I concentrate solely on language—vocabulary and authenticity. . . . The second pass consists of looking for all the tropes, metaphors, and similes in order to make sure they're integral to the story. Then, after letting it age a few days, I go through a third time and check all the punctuation and thin out anything extraneous. In the fourth pass I expand on the material still there. The final pass is an edit of anything that has been added. The process is a bit mechanical but very effective; it produces a clean manuscript."

Katie Bolick and David Watta, "A Conversation with Tim Gautreaux," *Atlantic Online,* March 14, 1997, http://www.theatlantic
.com/unbound/factfict/gautreau/tgautr.htm (accessed April 21,
2008); subsequent quotations from this interview will be cited parenthetically.

4. Gautreaux explained in his remarks about this story for its
reprint in *The Best American Short Stories 1992* that he too "realized, 'Hell, she killed him,'" only as he revised the story (in the first
draft, he says, the death was an accident): "This murder was what
everything, including her hard life, and her desires, pointed to." He
adds, "After finishing the tale, I realized that some of the best stories
come from attention to culture and history, and that no person and
no place, even the dull backwoods or the bland suburb is devoid of
those aspects." In Robert Stone and Katrina Kenison, eds., *The Best
American Short Stories 1992* (Boston: Houghton Mifflin, 1992),
368.

5. Ed Piacentino, "Second Chances: Patterns of Failure and
Redemption in Tim Gautreaux's *Same Place, Same Things*," *Southern Literary Journal* 38, no. 1 (2005): 116; subsequent quotations
from this essay will be cited parenthetically.

6. Kane also includes in this list of what distinguishes this story
from an O'Connor story "the female character who seems the
embodiment of the word 'toughness,' [and] the male character faced
with a difficult moral decision," but the confrontation between these
two characters over a moral dilemma is part of what brings O'Connor's "A Good Man Is Hard to Find" or "Good Country People" to
mind when one reads this Gautreaux story. Kane, "Tim Gautreaux,
1947– ," in *Twenty-First-Century American Novelists,* ed. Lisa
Abney and Suzanne Disheroon-Green, vol. 292 of *Dictionary of Literary Biography* (Detroit: Gale, 2004), http://galenet.galegroup.com/
servlet/LitRC?vrsn=3&OP=contains&locID=gree96177&srchtp=
athr&ca=1&c=1&ste=6&tab=1&tbst=arp&ai=U14676758&n=
10&docNum=H1200011638&ST=GAUTREAUX&bConts=2191/
(accessed May 21, 2008).

202 / Notes to Pages 20–51

7. L. Lamar Nisly, "A Sacramental Science Project in Tim Gautreaux's 'Resistance,'" *Logos: A Journal of Catholic Thought and
Culture* 5, no. 4 (2002): 139; subsequent quotations from this essay
will be cited parenthetically. In contrast to my reading here and to
Nisly's, Piacentino reads these same sentences as reflecting a more
negative interpretation of this story's ending, in which he sees Harry
also stuck in the rut alluded to in the title: "still in the same place,
[doing] the same things." Piacentino, "Second Chances," 117.

8. Julie Kane, "A Postmodern Southern Moralist and Storyteller
Tim Gautreaux," in *Voces de América: Entrevistas a escritores ameri-
canos / American Voices: Interviews with American Writers*, ed.
Laura P. Alonso Gallo (Cádiz, Spain: Aduana Vieja, 2004), 138; subsequent quotations from this essay will be cited parenthetically.

9. Christina Masciere, "Novel Approach: Tim Gautreaux Takes
'The Next Step,'" *New Orleans Magazine*, March 1998, 35; subsequent quotations from this interview will be cited parenthetically.

10. Ed Piacentino includes a discussion of this story in "Intersecting
Paths: The Humor of the Old Southwest as Intertext," his introductory essay to his edited collection on *The Enduring Legacy of Old
Southwest Humor* (Baton Rouge: Louisiana State University Press,
2006), 3–5.

11. Jennifer Levasseur and Kevin Rabalais, "Interview with Tim
Gautreaux," *Mississippi Review* 27, no. 3 (1999): 23; subsequent
quotations from this interview will be cited parenthetically.

12. L. Lamar Nisly, "Wingless Chickens or Catholics from the
Bayou: Conceptions of Audience in O'Connor and Gautreaux,"
Christianity and Literature 56, no. 1 (2006): 79.

13. Again this reading is more positive than Piacentino's. He perceives Felix at the end of the story "disillusioned and defeated, his
identity still defined only by his occupation as an exterminator,
his desire for reciprocation remaining elusive." Piacentino, "Second
Chances," 126.

14. E. Annie Proulx and Katrina Kenison, eds., *The Best American
Short Stories 1997* (Boston: Houghton Mifflin, 1997), 361.

15. Another effect of the multiple points of view in this story, according to Piacentino, is how it "accentuate[s] the strength and cohesion of the rural Cajun community." Piacentino, "Second Chances," 127.

16. Gautreaux goes a little further into the troubling subject of race relations with the plot surrounding the mixed-race housekeeper, May, and her "almost white" baby in his second novel, *The Clearing*, published after this interview.

Chapter 3—*The Next Step in the Dance*

Epigraph from Tim Gautreaux, *The Next Step in the Dance* (New York: Picador, 1998), 7; subsequent quotations from this novel will be cited parenthetically.

1. Margaret D. Bauer, "An Interview with Tim Gautreaux: 'Cartographer of Louisiana Back Roads,'" *Southern Spaces*, May 28, 2009, http://www.southernspaces.org/contents/2009/bauer/1a.htm (accessed May 28, 2009).

2. Julie Kane, "A Postmodern Southern Moralist and Storyteller Tim Gautreaux," in *Voces de América: Entrevistas a escritores americanos / American Voices: Interviews with American Writers*, ed. Laura P. Alonso Gallo (Cádiz, Spain: Aduana Vieja, 2004), 129–30; subsequent quotations from this essay will be cited parenthetically.

3. Tiger Island, the name of the town in which this novel is set (which also figures in *The Clearing* as the closest real community to that novel's swamp setting), is the original name for Morgan City, Gautreaux's hometown in Louisiana, known as "the gateway to the Gulf of Mexico for the shrimping and oilfield industries" (http://www.cityofmc.com/index.html; accessed May 20, 2009). Gautreaux told one book reviewer, however, that his fictional "Tiger Island is really a composite of three or four little towns—Morgan City . . . Donaldsonville, Houma and Thibodeaux." Susan Larson, "The Writer Next Door," *New Orleans Times-Picayune*, March 15, 1998, E1; subsequent quotations from this review will be cited parenthetically.

4. Tim Gautreaux, "Preface: Warts and All," in *New Stories from the South 2004: The Year's Best,* ed. Shannon Ravenel (Chapel Hill, N.C.: Algonquin, 2004), viii.

5. Gautreaux told Robert Birnbaum that the Los Angeles section of his novel, which he wrote about based upon spending summers with his sister in California, had originally been much longer, but his editor, a native of Los Angeles, found that section of the novel "unconvincing" and suggested he "trim it back." The writer expressed no regret for the lost section, and in this same interview he remarks upon writing about Louisiana, "The language of your region and all that is in your literary bones." Robert Birnbaum, "Interview: Tim Gautreaux," Identitytheory.com, October 1, 2003, http://www.identitytheory.com/interviews/birnbaum127.php (accessed November 28, 2007).

6. Colette's consideration of Bucky's appeal (and Bucky being a Texan) reminds the reader of the story "Floyd's Girl." When asked about his "'gendering' of this conflict"—that is, how the female character in several of his works, including these two, is the one who wants "to get out of south Louisiana, while the male lead characters seem to realize that place is central to their identities"—Gautreaux responds that "some of the women in my stories are a little rough around the edges, a little hardhearted. And to tell you the truth, a lot of rural women that I grew up with had to be pretty tough, intellectually and physically and emotionally, to survive the poverty and the rough men they'd married." Kane, "Postmodern," 133–34.

7. Julie Kane, "Tim Gautreaux, 1947– ," in *Twenty-First-Century American Novelists,* ed. Lisa Abney and Suzanne Disheroon-Green, vol. 292 of *Dictionary of Literary Biography* [Detroit: Gale, 2004], http://galenet.galegroup.com/servlet/LitRC?vrsn=3&OP=contains&locID=gree96177&srchtp=athr&ca=1&c=1&ste=6&tab=1&tbst=arp&ai=U14676758&n=10&docNum=H1200011638&ST=GAUTREAUX&bConts=2191/ (accessed May 21, 2008).

8. L. Lamar Nisly notes the "pivotal supporting role" that Abadie plays in the "healing" of this couple's relationship, linking Paul's

grandfather to other grandfather characters in Gautreaux's short stories. Nisly, "A Sacramental Science Project in Tim Gautreaux's 'Resistance,'" *Logos: A Journal of Catholic Thought and Culture* 5, no. 4 (2002): 140.

9. Maria Hebert-Leiter, "An Interview with Tim Gautreaux," *Carolina Quarterly* 57, no. 2 (2005): 73; subsequent quotations from this interview will be cited parenthetically.

10. Leonard Deutsch, "Cajun Culture: An Interview," *MELUS* 6, no. 1 (1979): 89. Again, whereas Gautreaux has remarked that he is "memorializ[ing]" with this novel the particular state "trauma" of the 1980s, the oil bust (Larson, "Writer Next Door," E1), one might also consider how his novel also provides an authentic view of Cajun culture in a time when "Cajun" cuisine, for example, was being bastardized all over the country. And Gautreaux does include a humorous scene in the novel in which Paul eats in a supposedly Cajun restaurant in California, complains about the food, and is told, "It takes time to develop a true Cajun palate," to which he responds, "It sure don't take much time to ruin one" (81).

11. Jennifer Levasseur and Kevin Rabalais, "Interview with Tim Gautreaux," *Mississippi Review* 27, no. 3 (1999): 31.

12. Christopher Scanlan, "Tim Gautreaux," *Creative Loafing Atlanta,* June 17, 2004, http://atlanta.creativeloafing.com/gyro base/tim_gautreaux/Content?oid=15955 (accessed November 28, 2007).

13. Susan Larson, "Pelican Briefs," *New Orleans Times-Picayune,* September, 15, 1996, D1.

Chapter 4—*Welding with Children*

Epigraph from Tim Gautreaux quoted in Margaret D. Bauer, "An Interview with Tim Gautreaux: 'Cartographer of Louisiana Back Roads,'" *Southern Spaces,* May 28, 2009, http://www.south ernspaces.org/contents/2009/bauer/1a.htm (accessed May 28, 2009); subsequent quotations from this interview will be cited parenthetically.

1. Tim Gautreaux, *Welding with Children* (New York: St. Martin's, 1999); quotations from this collection will be cited parenthetically.

2. Garrison Keillor and Katrina Kenison, eds., *The Best American Short Stories 1998* (Boston: Houghton Mifflin, 1998), 289.

3. L. Lamar Nisly, "Wingless Chickens or Catholics from the Bayou: Conceptions of Audience in O'Connor and Gautreaux," *Christianity and Literature* 56, no. 1 (2006): 69; subsequent quotations from this article will be cited parenthetically.

4. The examination of this story here has been adapted from my earlier discussion of it in my book *William Faulkner's Legacy: "what shadow, what stain, what mark"* (Gainesville: University Press of Florida, 2005), 186–91. After that book's publication, I asked Gautreaux if he had Faulkner's story in mind when he wrote this one, to which he responded, "I had in mind instead the archetype of the spinster lady left with the family house, which happens not only in the South but all over the place. You don't see it so much anymore because families now are composed of two kids. But say in the 1920s, a man would have a large house, and he would have six kids, and three of them would get married, one of them would get killed in a car accident or something, and then it seems like there was always one daughter that was left over; she never married, and she would wind up living in the father's house. . . . I knew a lot of women like this. . . . I even have a couple of them in my family. So that's where the archetype for that story came from. And that's probably the archetype that Faulkner drew on to write 'A Rose for Emily'" (Bauer, "Interview").

5. Jennifer Levasseur and Kevin Rabalais, "Interview with Tim Gautreaux," *Mississippi Review* 27, no. 3 (1999): 36.

6. Amy Tan and Katrina Kenison, eds., *The Best American Short Stories 1999* (Boston: Houghton Mifflin, 1999), 381.

7. Gautreaux agreed with this interpretation of events during my interview with him (Bauer, "Interview").

8. Indeed, in interviews Gautreaux talks both about encouraging his students to write what they know and about his own revising

method. See, for example, his *Atlantic Unbound* interview with Katie Bolick and David Watta ("A Conversation with Tim Gautreaux," *Atlantic Online,* March 14, 1997, http://www.theatlantic.com /unbound/factfict/gautreau/tgautr.htm; accessed April 21, 2008).

9. Christina Masciere, "Novel Approach: Tim Gautreaux Takes 'The Next Step,'" *New Orleans Magazine,* March 1998, 35.

10. Reading Mr. Boudreaux's contemplation on buying a new car similarly, L. Lamar Nisly suggests that "Mr. Boudreaux's thoughts here suggest more than a change in automobile; they imply that he is reconsidering his approach to those around him. Rather than resist the impersonality of his neighborhood, he seems to be thinking, perhaps he should simply accept the changed interactions between people; perhaps he should simply hole up in his house, live with his television and his memories, and allow the people around him to go on with their anonymous lives." L. Lamar Nisly, "A Sacramental Science Project in Tim Gautreaux's 'Resistance,'" *Logos: A Journal of Catholic Thought and Culture* 5, no. 4 (2002): 141; subsequent quotations from this essay will be cited parenthetically.

11. Erin McGraw, "Authoritative Voice," *Georgia Review* 54 (Winter 2000): 736.

12. Marc Fitten, "A Conversation with Tim Gautreaux," *Chattahoochee Review* 24, no. 1 (2003): 103.

Chapter 5—*The Clearing*

Epigraph from Tim Gautreaux, *The Clearing* (New York: Knopf, 2003), 256; subsequent quotations from this novel will be cited parenthetically.

1. Margaret D. Bauer, "An Interview with Tim Gautreaux: 'Cartographer of Louisiana Back Roads,'" *Southern Spaces,* May 28, 2009, http://www.southernspaces.org/contents/2009/bauer/1a.htm (accessed May 28, 2009). See also his discussion of his uncle's World War I experience in his interview with Marc Fitten, "A Conversation with Tim Gautreaux," *Chattahoochee Review* 24, no. 1 (2003): 103–4. Subsequent quotations from these two interviews will be cited parenthetically.

2. "Trying to go back to how it was" (8) is also why Byron listens over and over to the records he plays on his Victrola. As he further explains later on, the music takes him back to his earlier self: "It's those words I need. . . . They try to make me happy. . . . They nearly make me feel like when we were going out with the Wescott sisters" (114). But at the early point in the novel at which his brother arrives, he is not so successful. "This song. It used to be one way. Now it's another" (8), he says, suggesting that as a changed man, he cannot hear the music in the same way.

3. The reviewer for the *New Yorker* also sees this connection: "Gautreaux, like some Bayou Conrad, manages to combine verbal luxuriance and swift, brutal action to devastating effect." The Critics: Briefly Noted, *New Yorker,* June 30, 2003, 101.

4. In his interview with Jennifer Levasseur and Kevin Rabalais, Gautreaux comments on the variety of accents in his hometown of Morgan City and the different dialects found on opposite sides of some parishes. Levasseur and Rabalais, "Interview with Tim Gautreaux," *Mississippi Review* 27, no. 3 (1999): 21; subsequent quotations from this interview will be cited parenthetically.

5. Robert Birnbaum, "Interview: Tim Gautreaux," *Identity Theory*, October 1, 2003, http://www.identitytheory.com/interviews/birnbaum127.php (accessed November 28, 2007).

6. L. Lamar Nisly, "Presbyterian Pennsylvanians at a Louisiana Sawmill; or, Just How Catholic Is Gautreaux's *The Clearing*?" *U.S. Catholic Historian* 23, no. 3 (2005): 114.; subsequent references to this article will be cited parenthetically.

7. Also affected by war is the marshal, Merville, who was a boy during the Civil War: "He remembered living in a war, the one with the blue devils and the butternut devils riding back and forth through his father's sugar cane fields on Bayou Lafourche" (63). The imagery of his recollection suggests Merville's recognition that the soldiers of both sides of a war become "devils," and his son Minos's connection between the war experience in his father's youth and "getting raised by that old man was holy hell" also reflects the corrupting

consequences of war even to civilians, even to children. Minos tells Randolph, "I seen him be just like your brother, crying and breaking furniture" (147). Merville's choice of becoming a lawman, like Byron's, is connected to his war experience: when soldiers (whether Northern or Southern is not told) come through and threaten to kill members of the family if Merville's father does not tell them where he has hidden money, "Merville decided then that if he lived to be two hundred years old he would never be like these stinking outlaws, would never allow a kinked desire for blood to rise in him the way it did in these robbers' eyes before their weapons bucked and his father's fly-bled mule went down in its patched traces" (252). Killing the mule instead of family members is not unlike Crouch (also a veteran) putting the snake into the child's bed in the present of the novel: a form of slow killing that results in more suffering, since the mule is needed for them to farm and thus feed themselves.

8. Gautreaux, *Same Place, Same Things* (New York: St. Martin's, 1996), 151.

9. Weapons play a role in an interesting subplot of the novel involving the marshal, who as noted previously has also taken up arms in response to his war experience as a boy watching the effects of war on his family and on the soldiers who passed through, whether wearing blue or grey. Finally fed up with his ineffectuality against the mob, he deputizes Byron and Randolph and what men they are able to enlist to help in a kind of *High Noon* stand, but then Merville dies before they go into "battle" (though they hide the fact of his death and proceed with his plans). After things have settled down and they finally bury Merville, Minos, Merville's son, shows Randolph his father's arsenal of weapons confiscated from criminals over many years and thrown behind an armoire in his house. When they pull the armoire out from the wall, there is "an avalanche of weaponry so dense and dust-bound" that it takes Randolph a while to recognize what it is: "straight razors, skinning knives, spiked knuckles, break-action Smith & Wesson, Iver Johnson, Hopkins and Allen pistols, pocket shotguns, machetes, ice picks, hat knives,

cabbage knives, corkscrews, lever-action rifles, slapjacks, scalpels, pump guns, giant scissors, single-shot shotguns bound together with string and tape by men poor in everything but revenge, pieces of metal shaped to stab or slice, innocent pipe and tie-rod sharpened to death. . . . An arsenal . . . enough to equip a crazed, primal army. . . . With a shudder Randolph began to imagine all the things that had never happened" because Merville had confiscated these weapons (272–73).

10. See Nisly's article on *The Clearing* for a discussion of the relationship between and roles of the marshal and the priest in this novel (Nisly, "Presbyterian Pennsylvanians," 111–12). And see Gautreaux's interview in the *Chattahoochee Review* in which he says "the scariest line in the novel" is Buzetti's response to Byron's question, "'Why did we do it?' . . . 'Because somebody gave the permission. That's a great thing, permission. After the war, I learned to give it to myself'" (*Clearing*, 158). Gautreaux compares this attitude to "the standard operating procedure" of lawmen like Byron in a place like Nimbus in the 1920s (Fitten, "Conversation," 107).

11. Later, after leading (with Byron, Minos, and Merville's corpse) the mass arrest of the mob for smuggling liquor, which results in numerous deaths, Randolph tries to soothe his prickling conscience by escaping into a false sense of security, which he finds in this perception of himself as a cog in an invincible machine: "He was engaged like a machine in his mill, a moving part of the process leading from stump to farmstead in Minnesota. His work shut out worry, became again life's real adventure. He remained on his guard, but nothing could happen in the mill yard, which, after all, was being watched like a fortress" (275). In spite of or perhaps because of his complacence, Crouch sneaks in and shoots him just after this passage.

12. Elizabeth Schultz has noted a pattern in fiction by white writers in which a black character serves as either friend/confidant or mentor, helps to raise a white character's racial awareness, and then is deserted in the sense that the friendship becomes a mere memory to

the white protagonist, who goes on to live the rest of his/her life, enlightened perhaps, but no longer needing the black "friend" now that some crisis has passed. Elizabeth Schultz, "Out of the Woods and into the World: A Study of Interracial Friendships between Women in American Novels," in *Conjuring: Black Women, Fiction, and Literary Tradition*, ed. Marjorie Pryse and Hortense J. Spillers (Bloomington: Indiana University Press, 1985), 67–85. When asked about the rare occurrence of racial conflicts in fiction set in a state in which race is still very much an issue, Gautreaux responds, "I don't write about race. I write about people. . . . Let me tell you why nothing big in the way of racial stuff happens: always stick to the narrative. . . . The minute a writer says, 'I'm going to write about race' instead of 'I'm going to write a story about people' he has already failed." Gautreaux uses his next novel to illustrate his point: "The story of *The Missing* is driven by Sam's character, and his character involves him in this rescue search, and that's what the whole novel is going to be about" (Bauer, "Interview"). In *The Clearing*, the narrative is driven by Randolph and Byron's story, not May's—but also not the (white) marshal's, sheriff's, or priest's.

13. The novel also casts Randolph in the role of Lazarus, rising from his own deathbed after being touched by Byron, who becomes the Christ figure in this analogy: "The room came apart and drifted away, and Randolph prayed for forgiveness for whatever he'd done wrong in his life, and then suddenly, when he felt his brother's touch and voice, the walls came back together, light again registering in his brain and his eyes seeing as if through broken water" (284).

14. Nisly suggests that experiencing evil may also add a "spiritual depth" to Randolph that, as noted, he lacked at the novel's beginning (Nisly, "Presbyterian Pennsylvanians," 117). After the snake is put into the bed of his infant son, he is "suddenly aware of hell as a real possibility, for he had finally been touched by someone who might be deserving of it" (*Clearing*, 239). Nisly compares Randolph's realization to Flannery O'Connor's grandmother meeting the Misfit (Nisly, "Presbyterian Pennsylvanians," 116).

15. L. Lamar Nisly, "A Catholic Who Happens to Write: An Interview with Tim Gautreaux," *Interdisciplinary Literary Studies* 8, no. 2 (2007): 97.

Chapter 6—*The Missing*

Epigraph from Tim Gautreaux, *The Missing* (New York: Knopf, 2009), 6; subsequent quotations from this novel will be cited parenthetically.

1. Margaret D. Bauer, "An Interview with Tim Gautreaux: 'Cartographer of Louisiana Back Roads,'" *Southern Spaces,* May 28, 2009, http://www.southernspaces.org/contents/2009/bauer/1a.htm (accessed May 28, 2009).

Afterword

Epigraph from Tim Gautreaux quoted in L. Lamar Nisly, "A Catholic Who Happens to Write: An Interview with Tim Gautreaux," *Interdisciplinary Literary Studies* 8, no. 2 (2007): 93.

1. Leonard Deutsch, "Cajun Culture: An Interview," *MELUS* 6, no. 1 (1979): 89, 84.

2. Margaret Donovan Bauer, *William Faulkner's Legacy: "what shadow, what stain, what mark"* (Gainesville: University Press of Florida, 2005), 186.

3. Matthew Guin, *After Southern Modernism: Fiction of the Contemporary South* (Jackson: University Press of Mississippi, 2000), xiii.

4. Quoted in Robert Birnbaum, "Interview: Tim Gautreaux," Identitytheory.com, October 1, 2003, http://www.identitytheory.com/interviews/birnbaum127.php (accessed November 28, 2007).

Bibliography

Primary Works

Books by Gautreaux

The Clearing. New York: Knopf, 2003.

The Missing. New York: Knopf, 2009.

The Next Step in the Dance. New York: Picador, 1998.

Same Place, Same Things. New York: St. Martin's, 1996.

Welding with Children. New York: St. Martin's, 1999.

Stories by Gautreaux in Magazines and Anthologies

"The Bug Man." *GQ*, October 1994, 130–40. Reprinted in *New Stories from the South, 1995: The Year's Best*, 91–107 (Chapel Hill, N.C.: Algonquin Books, 1995).

"The Courtship of Merlin LeBlanc." *Louisiana Cultural Vistas* 7, no. 3 (1996): 52–63.

"Dancing with the One-Armed Gal." *Zoetrope* 3, no. 2 (1999): 24–31. Reprinted in *New Stories from the South, 2000: The Year's Best*, 56–77 (Chapel Hill, N.C.: Algonquin Books, 2000).

"Deputy Sid's Gift." *Harper's*, November 1995, 55–64. Reprinted in *A Very Southern Christmas: Holiday Stories from the South's Best Writers*, ed. Charline R. McCord and Judy H. Tucker, 15–34 (Chapel Hill: N.C.: Algonquin Books, 2003).

"Died and Gone to Vegas." *Atlantic*, February 1995, 75–86. Reprinted in *New Stories from the South, 1996: The Year's Best*, 170–89 (Chapel Hill, N.C.: Algonquin Books, 1996); *The Longman Anthology of Short Fiction: Stories and Authors in Context*, ed. Dana Gioia and R. S. Gwinn (New York: Longman, 2000); and The Best American Catholic Short Stories, ed. Daniel McVeigh and Patricia Schnapp, 291–306 (Lanham, Md.: Rowman & Littlefield, 2007).

"Easy Pickings." *GQ*, August 1999, 103–12. Reprinted in *Prize Stories 2000: The O. Henry Awards,* 287–99 (New York: Doubleday, 2000).

"Floyd's Girl." *Virginia Quarterly Review* 70, no. 2 (1994): 239–55.

"Good for the Soul." *Story* 47, no. 3 (1999): 34–47. Reprinted in *The Best American Short Stories 2000,* ed. E. L. Doctorow, 135–50 (Boston: Houghton Mifflin, 2000), and in *The Best American Catholic Short Stories,* ed. Daniel McVeigh and Patricia Schnapp, 291-306 (Lanham, Md.: Rowman & Littlefield, 2007).

"Idols." *New Yorker,* 22 June 2009, 70–79.

"Just Turn Like a Gear." *Massachusetts Review* 27 (1986): 5–32. Reprinted in *A Good Deal: Selected Stories from the Massachusetts Review,* ed. Mary Heath and Fred Miller Robinson, 17–40 (University of Massachusetts Press, 1988).

"License to Steal." *Crescent Review* 9, no. 1 (1991): 31–39.

"Little Frogs in a Ditch." *GQ,* March 1996, 142, 147–52. Reprinted in *The Best American Short Stories 1997,* ed. Annie Proulx, 335–48 (Boston: Houghton Mifflin, 1997), and in *New Stories from the South, 1997: The Year's Best,* 57–72 (Chapel Hill, N.C.: Algonquin Books, 1997).

"Misuse of Light." *New York Stories* 1, no. 3 (1999): 7–13.

"People on the Empty Road." *Story* 43 (1995): 21–36. Reprinted in *Stories from the Blue Moon Café III,* ed. Sonny Brewer, 151–72 (San Francisco: MacAdam/Cage, 2004).

"The Piano Tuner." *Harper's,* September 1998, 72–84. Reprinted in *The Best American Short Stories 1999,* ed. Amy Tan, 78–96 (Boston: Houghton Mifflin).

"The Pine Oil Writers Conference." *Image* 24 (1999): 47–58.

"Resistance." *Ploughshares* 23, nos. 2–3 (1997): 62–76.

"Rodeo Patrol." *Georgia Review* 52 (Winter 1998): 683–86. Reprinted in *Writers Harvest 3,* ed. Tobias Wolff, 113–18 (New York: Dell, 2000), and in *Voices of the American South,* ed. Suzanne Disheroon-Green, 1291–93 (New York: Pearson/Longman, 2005).

"A Sacrifice of Doves." *Kansas Quarterly* 15, no. 2 (1983): 173–81.

"The Safe." *Atlantic Monthly Fiction Issue* (September/October 2006), http://www.theatlantic.com/doc/200608/tim-gautreaux (accessed July 1, 2009). Reprinted in *New Stories from the South, 2007: The Year's Best,* 113–33 (Chapel Hill, N.C.: Algonquin Books, 2007).

"Same Place, Same Things." *Atlantic,* June 1991, 84–91. Reprinted in *The Best American Short Stories 1992,* ed. Robert Stone and Katrina Kennison, 94–109 (Boston: Houghton Mifflin, 1992), and in *Scribner Anthology of Contemporary Short Fiction: Fifty North American Stories since 1970,* ed. Lex Williford and Michael Martone (New York: Scribner Paperback Fiction, 1999).

"Something for Nothing." *Harper's,* September 2002, 66–72.

"Sorry Blood." *Fiction Magazine* 14, no. 2 (1997). Reprinted in *New Stories from the South, 1998: The Year's Best,* 169–86 (Chapel Hill, N.C.: Algonquin Books, 1998).

"Sunset in Heaven." *Epoch* 44, no. 3 (1995): 321–33.

"Waiting for the Evening News." *Story* 42 (1994): 104–17.

"Welding with Children." *Atlantic,* March 1997, 80–88. Reprinted in *The Best American Short Stories 1998,* edited by Garrison Keillor, 254–68 (Boston: Houghton Mifflin), and in *Wide Awake in the Pelican State: Stories by Contemporary Louisiana Writers,* ed. Ann Brewster Dobie, 200–213 (Baton Rouge: Louisiana State University Press, 2006).

Essays by Gautreaux

"Behind the Great Stories There Are Great Sentences." *Boston Globe,* October 19, 1997, 4.

"How Sweet It Was." *Preservation,* May/June 2005, 24–25.

"Hussy in the Hood." *Best of the Oxford American: Ten Years from the Southern Magazine of Good Writing,* edited by Mark Smirnoff, 118-25. (Athens, Ga: Hill Street Press, 2002)

"Left-Handed Love." In *A Few Thousand Words about Love,* edited by Mickey Pearlman, 127–42. New York: St. Martin's, 1998.

"Perfect Strangers on a Train." *Oxford American,* March–April 2000, 26–36.

"Preface: Warts and All." In *New Stories from the South, 2004: The Year's Best,* edited by Shannon Ravenel, vii–x. Chapel Hill, N.C.: Algonquin Books, 2004.

Secondary Bibliography

Articles

Kane, Julie. "Tim Gautreaux, 1947– ." In *Twenty-First-Century American Novelists,* edited by Lisa Abney and Suzanne Disheroon-Green, 119–25. Vol. 292 of *Dictionary of Literary Biography.* Detroit: Gale, 2004.

Nisly, L. Lamar. "Presbyterian Pennsylvanians at a Louisiana Sawmill, or Just How Catholic Is Gautreaux's *The Clearing?*" *U.S. Catholic Historian* 23, no. 3 (2005): 109–19.

———. "A Sacramental Science Project in Tim Gautreaux's 'Resistance.'" *Logos: A Journal of Catholic Thought and Culture* 5, no. 4 (2002): 135–51.

———. "Wingless Chickens or Catholics from the Bayou: Conceptions of Audience in O'Connor and Gautreaux." *Christianity and Literature* 56, no. 1 (2006): 63–85.

Piacentino, Ed. "Intersecting Paths: The Humor of the Old Southwest as Intertext." In *The Enduring Legacy of Old Southwest Humor,* edited by Ed Piacentino, 1–35. Baton Rouge: Louisiana State University Press, 2006.

———. "Second Chances: Patterns of Failure and Redemption in Tim Gautreaux's *Same Place, Same Things.*" *Southern Literary Journal* 38, no. 1 (2005): 115–33.

Interviews

Arnold, Elizabeth. "Best Short Stories 1997." *All Things Considered.* NPR, December 15, 1997.

Bauer, Margaret D. "An Interview with Tim Gautreaux: 'Cartographer of Louisiana Back Roads.'" *Southern Spaces,* May 28,

2009. http://www.southernspaces.org/contents/2009/bauer/1a .htm (accessed May 28, 2009).

Birnbaum, Robert. "Interview: Tim Gautreaux." Identitytheory.com. October 1, 2003. http://www.identitytheory.com/interviews/ birnbaum127.php (accessed November 28, 2007).

Bolick, Katie, and David Watta. "A Conversation with Tim Gautreaux." *Atlantic Online*, March 14, 1997. http://www.the atlantic.com/unbound/fact/fict/gautreau/tgautr.htm (accessed April 21, 2008).

Fitten, Marc. "A Conversation with Tim Gautreaux." *Chatta-hoochee Review* 24, no. 1 (2003): 103–12.

Hebert-Leiter, Maria. "An Interview with Tim Gautreaux." *Carolina Quarterly* 57, no. 2 (2005): 66–74.

Joyal, Christopher. "An Interview with Tim Gautreaux." *New Delta Review* 16, no. 1 (1998): 87–97.

Kane, Julie. "A Postmodern Southern Moralist and Storyteller Tim Gautreaux." In *Voces de América: Entrevistas a escritores ameri-canos / American Voices: Interviews with American Writers*, edited by Laura P. Alonso Gallo, 123–45. Cadiz, Spain: Aduana Vieja, 2004.

Kingsbury, Pam. "'Everything Has a Purpose': An Interview with Tim Gautreaux." *Southern Scribe* 4, no. 8 (2003). http://www .southernscribe.com/zine/authors/Gautreaux_Tim.htm (accessed November 28, 2007).

Langley, Greg. "Gautreaux Doesn't Need a Label Other Than 'Writer.'" *Baton Rouge Advocate*, October 10, 1999, 11–12.

Larson, Susan. "Pelican Briefs." *New Orleans Times-Picayune*, Sep-tember 15, 1996, D1.

Levasseur, Jennifer, and Kevin Rabalais. Interview. *Mississippi Review* 27, no. 3 (1999): 19–40.

Masciere, Christina. "Novel Approach: Tim Gautreaux Takes 'The Next Step.'" *New Orleans Magazine*, March 1998, 31, 35, 47.

Nisly, L. Lamar. "A Catholic Who Happens to Write: An Interview with Tim Gautreaux." *Interdisciplinary Literary Studies* 8, no. 2 (2007): 92–99.

Scanlan, Christopher. "Tim Gautreaux." *Creative Loafing Atlanta,* June 17, 2004. http://atlanta.creativeloafing.com/gyrobase/tim _gautreaux/Content?oid=15955; (accessed May 7, 2009).

Selected Reviews

Same Place, Same Things

Berne, Suzanne. "Swamped." *New York Times Book Review,* September 22, 1996, 16.

Cooper, Rand Richards. "Local Color." *Commonweal,* November 8, 1996, 24–25.

Elmore, Alice Lankford. "Books about the South." *Southern Living,* October 1996, 108.

Glasser, Perry. "True Dirt." *North American Review,* March–April 1997, 43–45.

Kirkus Reviews. September 11, 1996, 991.

Larson, Susan. "First, You Make a Roux." *New Orleans Times-Picayune,* September 15, 1996, E7.

McCay, Mary. "Men in Shorts." *New Orleans Review* 22, nos. 3–4 (1996): 181–85.

Notes on Current Books. *Virginia Quarterly Review* 73, no. 2 (1997): 57.

O'Laughlin, Jim. Untitled review. *Booklist,* September 1, 1996, 61.

Williams, Wilda. Untitled review. *Library Journal,* September 1, 1996, 213.

The Next Step in the Dance

Caso, Frank. Untitled review. *Booklist* 94, nos. 9–10 (1998): 774.

Larson, Susan. "The Writer Next Door." *New Orleans Times-Picayune,* March 15, 1998, E1.

Solomon, Andy. Books in Brief: Fiction. *New York Times Book Review,* June 14, 1998, 21.

Tait, John. *Missouri Review* 21, no. 2 (1998): 212.

Welding with Children

Balée, Susan. "Maximalist Fiction." *Hudson Review* 53, no. 3 (2000): 513–20.

Callanan, Liam. "La. Stories." *New York Times Book Review,* October 3, 1999, 31.

Heathcock, Alan. Book Reviews. *Mid-American Review* 20 (2000): 249–51.

Langley, Greg. "Short Stories Long on Understanding: Hammond Author Finds Inspiration in the Events of Everyday Life." *Baton Rouge Advocate,* October 10, 1999, 11–12.

McGraw, Erin. "Authoritative Voice." *Georgia Review* 54 (Winter 2000): 727–37.

Wanner, Irene. "An Imaginative Teller of Tales." *Seattle Times,* October 10, 1999. http://community.seattletimes.nwsource.com/archive/?date=19991010&slug=2987981 (accessed May 26, 2009).

The Clearing

Charles, Ron. "The Hard Struggle to Be a Brother's Keeper." *Christian Science Monitor,* July 24, 2003. http://www.csmonitor.com/2003/0724/p18s02-bogn.html (accessed May 26, 2009).

Cohu, Will. "The Wilderness Years." *Telegraph* (London), September 21, 2003. http://www.telegraph.co.uk/culture/books/3603061/The-wilderness-years.html (accessed May 26, 2009).

Cox, Rosemary. "Damnation and Redemption in Tim Gautreaux's *The Clearing.*" *Chattahoochee* 24, no. 1 (2003): 113–16.

The Critics: Briefly Noted. *New Yorker,* June 30, 2003, 101.

deFalbe, John. "Dark Satanic Mill." *Spectator,* October 4, 2003, 56.

Donovan, Deborah. "War's Hidden Costs." BookPage.com. 2003. http://www.bookpage.com/0307bp/fiction/clearing.html (accessed May 7, 2009).

Folks, Jeffrey J. Untitled review. *World Literature Today* 78, nos. 3–4 (2004): 93.

Minzesheimer, Bob. "*Clearing* Is a Cut Above." *USA Today,* July 31, 2003. http://www.usatoday.com/life/books/reviews/2003-07-23-clearing_x.htm (accessed May 7, 2009).

Poster, Jem. "Something Stirred." *Guardian Unlimited,* October 18, 2003. http://www.guardian.co.uk/books/2003/oct/18/featuresreviews.guardianreview19 (accessed May 26, 2009).

PW Forecasts: Fiction. *Publishers Weekly,* May 26, 2003, 49.

Salter, Kate. Untitled review. *Times Literary Supplement,* December 2003, 27.

Spencer, Jamie. "Human Depravity and Primordial Wood Cut in *The Clearing.*" *St. Louis Post-Dispatch,* June 29, 2003. http://www.stltoday.com/stltoday/entertainment/reviews.nsf/Book/150D356AE32F727486256D520071BB3C?OpenDocument&Headline=Human+depravity+and+primordial+wood+cut+in+%22The+Clearing%22/ (accessed April 28, 2008).

Temes, Peter. "Bayou Boon Troubles Shattered War Vet." *San Francisco Chronicle,* July 6, 2003, M3.

Weaver, Rebecca. "Heirs of History." *Ruminator Review* 15 (2003): 49.

Wilson, Robert. "Fellers and Sawyers." *New York Times Book Review,* September 21, 2003, 19.

The Missing

Charles, Ron. "On the Wide Mississippi, a Child Goes Missing." *Washington Post,* March 11, 2009, C4.

Childers, Doug. "The Persistence of Memories." *Richmond Times-Dispatch,* April 28, 2009. http://www.timesdispatch.com/rtd/entertainment/books_literature/article/BMISS22_20090318-192903/235128/ (accessed April 28, 2009).

Grimm, Fred. "A Crime Novel, but Better." *Raleigh News & Observer,* March 22, 2009, D9.

Larson, Susan. "Novelist Tim Gautreaux Is River Bound in *The Missing,*" *New Orleans Times Picayune,* March 11, 2009. http://blog.nola.com/susanlarson/2009/03/novelist_tim_gautreaux_is_rive.html#more (accessed March 13, 2009).

Leddy, Chuck. "Currents of Loss and Revenge Run Deep in *The Missing.*" *Boston Globe,* April 16, 2009. http://www.boston.com/ae/books/articles/2009/04/16/currents_of_loss_and_revenge_run_deep_in_the_missing/ (accessed April 28, 2009).

Maury, Laurel. Untitled review. *San Francisco Chronicle,* April 9, 2009, E3.

Payne, Tom. "*The Missing* by Tim Gautreaux: Review." *Telegraph* [London], April 24, 2009. http://www.telegraph.co.uk/culture/books/bookreviews/5208076/The-Missing-by-Tim-Gautreaux-review.html (accessed April 28, 2009).

Simon, Clea. "River Song: A Lyrical Turn in the South." *Boston Phoenix*, May 13, 2009. http://thephoenix.com/Boston/Arts/82843–River-song/ (accessed May 22, 2009).

Urquhart, James. "*The Missing* by Tim Gautreaux." *Independent* [U.K.], April 20, 2009. http://www.independent.co.uk/arts-entertainment/books/reviews/the-missing-by-tim-gautreaux-1671220.html (accessed April 28, 2009).

Warner, Alan. "River of Blood." *Guardian* [London], April 11, 2009. http://www.guardian.co.uk/books/2009/apr/11/the-missing-gautreaux-review (accessed April 28, 2009).

Watrous, Malena. "Absence and Malice." *New York Times Book Review*, April 5, 2009, 14.

Index

230 / Index